WHAT'S SO AMAZING ABOUT POLAR BEARS?

What's SO AMAZING about Polar Bears?

Teaching Kids to Care for Creation

RANDY HAMMER

KRISTIN HAMMER EVANS

SUZANNE BLOKLAND

THE PILGRIM PRESS

CLEVELAND

The Pilgrim Press, 700 Prospect Avenue, Cleveland, Ohio 44115
thepilgrimpress.com
© 2011 by Randy Hammer, Kristin Hammer Evans, Suzanne Blokland

15   14   13   12   11   5   4   3   2   1

Library of Congress Cataloging-in-Publication Data

Hammer, Randy, 1955–
    What's so amazing about polar bears? : teaching kids to care for creation / Randy Hammer, Kristin Hammer Evans, Suzanne Blokland.
        p. cm.
    Includes bibliographical references.
    ISBN 978-0-8298-1877-2 (alk. paper)
    1. Human ecology—Religious aspects—Christianity—Study and teaching.   2. Christian education of children.   I. Evans, Kristin Hammer, 1980– II. Blokland, Suzanne, 1965– III.   Title.
BT695.5.H353 2011
261.8'8—dc23   2011031586

Contents

Introduction

HOW TO USE THIS RESOURCE

What's So Amazing about Polar Bears? is an interactive Christian-based curriculum containing six lessons that can be used as a resource for Sunday school, Sunday evening or midweek activity, Vacation Bible School, or outdoor camp. Each lesson has an ecology theme with a scriptural background for study, reflection, and discussion; fun facts relevant to the topic; experiential activities to engage the children and reinforce the lesson; story options; suggested music and resources for further study; lists of supplies needed; and a concluding prayer. This resource will encourage children to learn, discover, experience, create, appreciate, respect, and help protect the amazing creation of which they are a part.

Each lesson contains a wealth of information and resources—from the very simple and adaptable that are easy to plan and implement for shorter time frames, to the more advanced for longer time frames and for those who are technically minded. Generally speaking, the lessons begin with suggested traditional studies and discussions and then move to experiential activities that can be planned outdoors, if desired. However, most of the material is suitable for use both indoors and out, depending on the setting. Leaders may pick and choose the materials and activities that best suit their situation, time frame, and resources. One could spend multiple weeks of one-hour sessions from each lesson, or have enough in each lesson to fill an entire day of activities, as in the case of daylong camp settings. What makes this work unique is the experiential nature of most of the activities and the vast offering of resources from which leaders may choose.

This resource may be used with elementary age children assigned to small groups (six to eight children with at least one adult leader) that experience the activities and lessons together all week, or children may roam at will from one activity to another, depending on setup. We encourage leaders to do what works best for them.

HELPFUL TIPS

About the Literature

Each lesson incorporates at least one children's book. If your public library does not have the book, ask the librarian to secure it through interlibrary loan or to suggest alternate titles.

About the Activities

Depending on your situation, you may have children in a wide range of developmental stages and a variety of learning styles. While some children may be able to sit and do crafts, others may need to move. Try to incorporate at least one activity that involves movement from each lesson. General precautions: Always use child-safe scissors and exercise caution when children are using them. Also, unless otherwise specified, use washable school glue.

Suggested Amount of Time for Activities

The suggested amount of time for activities often follows in parenthesis to help leaders plan and manage their time.

ONE

Amazement for God's Creation

THEME OF THE DAY
Wonder for creation

VERSE OF THE DAY
God saw everything that God had made, and, indeed, it was very good.
(Genesis 1:31)

PURPOSE OF THE LESSON
To nurture the child's innate curiosity and wonder of the
natural world. The writers believe that children will embrace caring
for the environment more readily if they first love it.

FOR THE LEADER—AN OPENING MEDITATION

Amazement. Utter amazement! Who has not experienced such amazement and awe when contemplating the wonders of creation? From watching a beautiful butterfly flit from flower to flower, or the hovering of the graceful hummingbird searching for nectar, or the long-necked giraffe stretching to munch on high branches, to the thunder of a waterfall as it cascades off a mountain—the wonders of creation never cease to amaze and move us to praise God, the Spirit of creation.

Psalm 148, a point of departure for today's study, is one of the most beautiful of the psalms that were written as songs of praise for the faith community in temple worship. This psalm also inspired the joyful hymn attributed to Francis of Assisi, "All Creatures of Our God and King." What better way to begin the day than to reflect upon those stirring words?

All creatures of our God and King,
Lift up your voice and with us sing
Alleluia, Alleluia!
Thou burning sun with golden beam,
Thou silver moon with softer gleam,
O praise him, O praise him,
Alleluia, Alleluia, Alleluia!

So let's get started being amazed at God's wonderful creation!

GATHERING TIME

Gathering Music

"To You, O God, All Creatures Sing" (*New Century Hymnal* #17) or another familiar hymn

Materials

- CD player and CD of "All Creatures of Our God and King" or "This Is My Father's World"

- computer with Internet capabilities, if possible

- YouTube video of "All Creatures of Our God and King" (http://www.youtube .com/watch?v=hD2i6Ymrxwg has an abundance of earth's creatures set to a traditional singing of "All Creatures of Our God and King")

- the book *Round Like a Ball* if the Internet or video are not available

If Internet is not available, consider playing a slideshow of nature images while playing one of the suggested hymns.

Advance Preparations

1. Provide seating, either a large rug or chairs, for the large group and small groups.

2. Have suggested materials ready to use.

3. Write the verse of the day on a large sheet of paper and hang for all to see.

GETTING STARTED (5–10 minutes)

Consider having one of the hymns suggested above softly playing as children gather.

Once children are gathered and seated, welcome them to the circle. Introduce yourself and the purpose of the day. Play the suggested YouTube video.

If Internet or video capabilities are not an option, read the children's book *Round Like a Ball* by Lisa Campbell Ernst.

Divide children into small groups for Sharing Time and Activity Time.

SHARING TIME

(Children may be divided into small groups.)

Materials

- books from the local library (find books and read about authors/artists):

  The Portfolios of Ansel Adams, Yosemite, Yosemite and the Range of Light, or *Yosemite and the High Sierra* by Ansel Adams

  Vincent van Gogh: *Van Gogh: The Complete Paintings* by Ingo F. Walther and Rainer Metzger or *Vincent van Gogh: The Starry Night* by Richard Thomson

  Thank You, World by Alice B. McGinty, illustrated by Wendy Anderson Halperin

  The Sun in Me: Poems about the Planet compiled by Judith Nicholls, illustrated by Beth Krommes

  Art catalogue books by Richard Thomson about various artists (visit Amazon's Richard Thomson "Author Page") (optional)

- Bibles
- poster board
- copies of questions
- prompts for Bible study

- pictures of creation
- paints, markers, or crayons and something to draw or paint on
- paper and pencils for writing
- flower pots, small stones, gardening soil, and small plants and grasses

A. SHARING THE LOVE OF CREATION

Sharing My Life (5–10 minutes)

Preparation

Prior to small group, think of a time when you remember seeing something beautiful in nature that amazed you, from the simple, like a sunset, to the miraculous, like the birth of an animal. Think of details to help children visualize your experience. Think how it made you feel to see this part of nature and how you responded.

Opening Small Group Questions

Share your experience with your small group. Then give the children an opportunity to share their own experiences. The following questions may help:

1. Think of a time you remember seeing something in nature that amazed you (it could have been a beautiful landscape, witnessing the birth of an animal, a waterfall, mountains, playing at the ocean, etc.). What was this experience like?
2. Where were you?
3. What happened?
4. What was so amazing about it?
5. How did it make you feel to see that part of nature?
6. What did this experience in nature make you want to do?

Sharing Others' Experiences of God's Creation (15–30 minutes)

Experiences of the natural world can lead people to express their feelings through art, songs, and other creative works. We will first explore examples of this in contemporary works of art.

We suggest that leaders choose one or two of the activities below, perhaps one picture and one book. Each small group can rotate from activity to activity together as a group.

For each work of art or literature, guide the discussion with children by moving from what the piece is about to what feelings the artist or writer may have had. Finally, ask the children how the piece makes them feel.

Say, "Sometimes when a person has an amazing experience or strong feelings about something, it inspires that person to share his or her experience with other people through a work of art like a drawing, painting, photograph, song, or poem. Often an artist will put feelings into the work of art. Let's take a look at some works of art about creation."

Ansel Adams' image *Nevada Fall, Rainbow*

1. What is this photo about?

2. What do you see?

3. Does anything in the picture stand out to you?

4. Why do you think the photographer, Ansel Adams, wanted to take a picture of this scene?

5. What feeling do you think he had about this scene?

6. How do you think seeing this scene in person would make you feel?

Vincent van Gogh's painting *Starry Night*

1. What do you see in this painting?

2. What do you think is the most important part that the artist wanted us to look at? (the stars)

3. Why do you think that? (The stars occupy a large portion of the canvas. Van Gogh used bright colors, with excited, swirling brushstrokes.)

4. How do you think the artist felt about stars? (Possibly he felt amazed, happy, awed when he looked at the night sky.)

5. How does this painting make you feel?

Alice B. McGinty's book *Thank You, World*

1. What kinds of things does the author talk about in the book?

2. How does the author feel about all the things in the world?

3. How does this book make you feel about the earth?

Mary Kawena Pukui's poem "Behold" (found in *The Sun in Me* poems, compiled by Judith Nicholls and illustrated by Beth Krommes)

1. What is this poem about?

2. What feeling do you think the author of this poem was experiencing?

3. How does this poem make you feel?

4. When you look at the world, what makes you think happy thoughts?

5. If you could be any animal or plant in the world, what would you be?

B. DISCOVERING THE PSALMIST'S EXPERIENCE OF GOD'S CREATION (15–30 minutes)

Note: Children may benefit from visuals that correspond to the verses. Find or draw pictures of the sun, moon, stars, earth, oceans, giant squid, lightning, hail, snow, clouds, hills, mountains, fruit trees, forests, animals, reptiles, birds. Also have pictures of things that wouldn't belong in these verses, like TVs, cars, and other modern, manufactured things.

Spread the pictures out where the children can see them while you read. When you mention one, they can raise their hands and you can call on a child to point out the picture. You can then tape it to the poster board.

Say, "Some of the verses in the Bible are like these paintings and songs and poems. They were written by someone who may have had an experience or feelings the writer wanted to share. Let's read a few verses from the Bible and talk about what you think they are about and what feelings the writer may have had." (Explain to your group how to find the book of Psalms by opening to the middle of the Bible or looking in the Table of Contents and how to turn to the chapters and verses.)

Read Psalm 148:1–12 as a group.

Questions for Discussion

1. What is the psalm about?
2. Can you imagine how the writer felt when writing this?
3. Why do you think the psalmist felt this way?
4. Why do you think that thinking about creation made the psalmist want to praise God?
5. Have you ever felt this way about nature or God?
6. Why do you think God made creation so amazing and beautiful?
7. How does this psalm make you want to respond?

C. ENCOURAGING CHILDREN'S CREATIVITY (15–30 minutes)

At this point, children may be ready and eager to express their own creative feelings artistically. Remember, some children will work quickly and others will take a long time. Some may want to draw or paint a picture, others create something with words, and others to work directly with the earth. Three art stations could be set up so as to give children the choice of one, two, or all three activities.

Paint a Picture

Encourage children to draw or paint a picture expressing their feelings about some aspect of creation.

Create a Garden

Assist children in creating a miniature garden with soil, small stones, small plants and grasses, and a pot.

Write a Poem or Story

For those children who enjoy words, provide encouragement to write a short poem or short essay on the wonder of creation (perhaps a poem about a bird, insect, or flower). The Japanese poetry form haiku is an unrhymed verse having a fixed, three-line format consisting of five, seven, and five syllables, respectively.

ACTIVITY TIME

Effective conservation efforts will depend, in part, on a lifestyle change of many individuals. Before such a dramatic shift can occur, people need to be aware of what's at stake. The goal of the following activities is to begin to raise awareness in children by introducing them to a few of earth's fascinating creatures.

A. WHAT'S SO AMAZING ABOUT THE BLUE WHALE? (10–15 minutes)

Purpose

To help children grasp how enormous the blue whale is

Materials

- 100-foot rope
- thick dowel rod, long enough to roll the rope on
- duct tape
- masking tape
- permanent marker
- index cards
- a space long enough to unroll 100 feet of rope
- pictures of the blue whale and the animals in the following list, if possible

FUN FACT: ONE OF THE SMALLEST LIVING ANIMALS IN THE WORLD IS THE MALE PARASITIC WASP, MEASURING ONLY 139 MICROMETERS IN LENGTH, AND ONE OF THE LARGEST AND LONGEST LIVING THINGS IS THE SEQUOIA TREE, WHICH CAN GROW UP TO 379 FEET (115 METERS) TALL AND LIVE 2,200 YEARS!

Advance Preparation

Mark the rope at the following lengths: 1 foot, 6½ feet, 10 feet, 12 feet, 32 feet, and 43 feet.

Tape one end of the rope to the dowel rod, with the 1-foot mark at the opposite end, then wrap the rest of the rope around it. Also, tape the ends of the rod to help protect children's hands.

On each index card, write the name and length of one of the animals below, so that each card has a different name on it. For ease of use, number the cards, with the seahorse being 1 and the giant squid being 6.

1. seahorse—1 foot (longest variety)
2. leatherback sea turtle—6½ feet
3. octopus (common Atlantic)—10 feet
4. bottlenose dolphin—up to 12 feet
5. killer whale—up to 32 feet
6. giant squid—43 feet

Procedure

Tell the children, "The blue whale is a really big animal and we're going to do an activity to find out how big it really is."

Pick two or three children to guess how long the whale is. Give each of them a piece of masking tape and take a piece for yourself.

Put your masking tape at one end of the room and tell the children, "This piece of tape marks one end of the whale. Now, the children with tape are going to put their pieces where they think the other end of the whale would be."

Once the tape has been put on the floor, select two more children to help unroll the rope and select six children to hold the index cards for placement. Tell the children, "As we unroll this rope, you will see marks on it. Each mark is the length of a different animal. When you see a mark, let me know."

Have one child hold the loose end of the rope on the floor at the masking tape marking one end of the whale. Let the other child hold the dowel rod and slowly unroll the rope. As the children find the marks on the rope, let the children with index cards place them in the appropriate spot (beginning with the card marked "1").

When you get to the giant squid, stop unrolling and let the children look at their guesses for how long the blue whale is. Tell them, "The giant squid is really big, but the blue whale is even bigger." If any of the tape pieces put down earlier are smaller than the giant squid, give the children a chance to put their tape in a new place. Then let the children continue to unroll the rope, slowly, until they get to the end.

Tell the children, "The blue whale can be as long as this whole piece of rope. That's 100 feet! Did you know that scientists think that this is the largest animal that has ever lived? Wow!" (Optional) Leave the rope on the floor and have the children lie down next to it so that they stretch out the entire length of the rope. How many children does it take to equal the length of one whale?

B. WHAT'S SO AMAZING ABOUT POLAR BEARS? (15–30 minutes)

Purpose

To help children grasp how well adapted the polar bear is to its very extreme environment by dressing their own human model with items that represent those adaptations

Materials

The following supplies are suggestions; feel free to improvise:

- paper cone with two holes cut opposite each other on one end
- two pieces of string long enough to tie the paper cone around model's face
- two clothespins
- safety goggles or swim goggles
- four cotton balls
- masking tape

- two paper plates
- two plastic forks
- two pieces of sandpaper, smaller than the paper plates
- 1-foot ruler
- bubble wrap
- black garbage bag (CAUTION: Do not allow children to put plastic bags over their heads, as suffocation may occur.)
- towel (white is preferable)
- large safety pins
- drinking straws or coffee stirrers (at least one per child)
- tail-shaped piece of paper, roughly an oval about 3½ inches long

Note: As you guide the children through each feature, remember that your own enthusiasm and amazement will help fuel the same feelings in children.

Procedure

In this activity, you will turn a person, either a child or an adult, into a polar bear model. Share each fact with the children (Fact), then help them add features to the model to mimic the polar bear (Act).

If you have a large group, put children in pairs. Each pair can read a fact and add an item to the model. Have the facts written on index cards.

FACT: The polar bear's snout is long, which helps warm the cold, Arctic air the bear inhales. The nose closes automatically when the bear is underwater. The polar bear has a better sense of smell than other bears and can smell food many miles away or three feet under snow and ice.
ACT: Tie the paper cone over the nose of your model (CAUTION: before putting the cone on the model, snip the tip of the cone with scissors to make a hole at least one inch wide. This lets the model breathe.)

FACT: The polar bear has extra, transparent eyelids that close automatically when the bear dives. When the bear is in the water, these eyelids protect its eyes and give it good vision.
ACT: Put on the safety goggles.

FACT: Polar bear ears are small, with fur inside, which helps conserve body heat. Like the nose, the ear canals close when the bear dives, to keep the water out.

ACT: Tape cotton balls to the strap of the safety goggles near the model's ears, then add a clothespin to the strap. Clothespins will hurt a person's ear, so don't put them on the real ear.

FACT: Have any of you ever been ice skating or tried to walk on ice? (Give children a chance to respond and talk about their experiences. Make sure they understand how difficult it is to walk on slippery ice.)

Polar bears have to travel across the snow and ice, but they don't fall down like we do because they have special feet. Their feet are really big. They can be as big across as a ruler. (Show the children the ruler and hold your hand over it to compare.) They also have webbing between the toes. These big feet act like snow shoes and keep the bear from sinking into the snow, and the webbing helps them paddle faster through the water

ACT: Tape the paper plates to the palms of the model's hands.

FACT: Each paw has five toes and each toe has a claw that is thick and curved and doesn't retract. (You may need to explain this term. You can compare it to a cat's claw, which does retract.) These claws help the bear grab onto the ice when it is running or climbing.

ACT: Tape the forks to the plates so that the tines extend over the edge.

FACT: The bottom of the bear's foot has little bumps and fur that also help keep the bear from slipping.

ACT: Tape the sandpaper to the bottom of the plates. Tape the cotton balls next to the sandpaper.

Ask the children: Do you ever feel cold? (Let them talk briefly about this.) Do you think you could play outside in the middle of winter, wearing short pants and a t-shirt? (Lead children to the idea that they need to wear warm clothes in the winter to keep from getting cold.)

As you know, polar bears live up near the North Pole. It's really, really cold there. But they don't get cold, even if the temperature drops to more than 30 degrees below zero. That's because they have several different kinds of coverings over their body.

FACT: Under their skin, polar bears have a layer of blubber, which is fat that keeps them warm. It can be more than four inches thick.

ACT: Wrap a layer of bubble wrap around torso of model and tape.

FACT: Their skin is thick and black. The black color absorbs energy from sunlight to warm them.
ACT: Wrap the black garbage bag around bubble wrap and tape it.

FACT: They have two kinds of fur. The under layer of fur is really thick and woolly and traps air next to the skin.
ACT: Wrap a towel around the garbage bag and tape or secure with safety pins.

FACT: The outer layer of fur is made of guard hair, which are like tiny, hollow tubes. They help keep the bear warm because they can trap heat and because they shed water, so the bear can shake off water and ice after swimming.
ACT: Let each child tape a drinking straw to the towel.

FACT: And last, but not least, is the tail, which is short on the polar bear. Like the small ears, this short length helps conserve body heat.
ACT: Tape the tail to the bottom of the towel.

Your model has been a good sport. Be sure that he or she takes a bow and gets a round of applause!

C. WHAT'S SO AMAZING ABOUT HUMMINGBIRDS? (10–15 minutes)

Purpose

To introduce children to some of the fascinating features of the tiny hummingbird

Materials

(for each child)

- a handful of beans
- paper towel tubes or stethoscopes (one for each pair of children)
- play dough (recipe for homemade at the end of the activity)
- cereal flakes (like corn flakes)
- cotton ball (several children can use one ball)
- thread (white mimics spider webs)
- two small white beans

(for the group)

- stopwatch or clock with second hand
- kitchen scale (if you have a scale that can measure grams, that would be great)
- bathroom scale
- apple (but any food will do)
- poster board (optional)
- marker (optional)

Note: Each hummingbird Fact/Act can be set up as a separate station. You can write the facts on poster board for children to read, then guide them through the activity.

Procedure

First, read a fact (Fact) to the children and explain, if necessary, then follow with the activity (Act).

FACT: Hummingbirds can beat their wings sixty to eighty times per second! Hummingbirds are also the only birds whose wings rotate in a circle. This enables them to fly forward and backwards. They can also fly up, down, and sideways. They can hover in one spot. And they can even fly upside down for a little while.

ACT: (You will use the stopwatch or clock with second hand for this act.) If a hummingbird can beat its wings sixty times in one second, this is equal to six hundred beats in ten seconds. Flap your arms as fast as you can while someone keeps time for ten seconds. How many times did you flap?

FACT: The smallest hummingbird, called the bee hummingbird of Cuba, is about 2 ¼ inches long and weighs only 2.2 grams (that's less than one tenth of an ounce).

ACT: Your scale probably isn't sensitive enough to measure one tenth of an ounce, but it should measure one ounce. Pour beans onto the scale until you have one ounce of beans. Divide those beans into ten piles, so that each group is approximately a tenth of an ounce. One pile weighs about the same as the smallest hummingbird.

FACT: A hummingbird may eat up to three times its weight in a day.

ACT: Do you think you could eat three times your weight in one day? Find out how much that would be. First, step on the bathroom scale and see how much you weigh.

Then weigh the apple on the kitchen scale. How many apples would you have to eat to equal three times your weight?

For example, if you weigh fifty pounds, you would have to eat 150 pounds to equal three times your weight. If an apple weighs half a pound, you would have to eat three hundred apples! *Note:* This math will be too complicated for younger children, so just help them understand how many apples they would have to eat. Older children can be encouraged to try to figure it out, with help from an adult.

Helpful Hint: Use a food that you have weighed ahead of time. Try to find a food with an easy to convert weight, such as a quarter pound, half pound, or one pound.

FACT: A hummingbird's heart can beat five hundred times in one minute.

ACT: How does your heart rate compare to that of a hummingbird? Find a partner and listen to each other's heartbeats. Put the paper towel tube end on the center of your partner's chest. Can you hear the heart beat? Once you can, have someone time you for one minute while you count the number of beats.

FACT: A hummingbird nest is really tiny, about the size of half of a ping-pong ball. The female builds the nest, covering the outer part with moss and plant fibers and camouflaging it with lichen. The inside may be lined with plant down and spider webs.

ACT: The female hummingbird will take days to build the nest, but you can build a model much more quickly.

1. Take a small ball of play dough and push your thumb into it and shape it into a bowl about the size of half of a ping-pong ball.

2. Break the cereal flakes into smaller pieces, if necessary, and press them onto the outside of the bowl. This is like the lichen the hummingbird uses.

3. Pull the cotton ball apart and use the fluff to line the nest. This is like plant down. The nest can also be lined with the thread, which is like the spider web silk.

4. Place two small beans in the nest. These represent the eggs.

5. If you want, you can make a hummingbird mother and set her on the eggs. Remember, her beak is long and thin.

6. Let the dough dry before the children take it home.

Dough Recipe:

2 cups flour
2 cups water
1 cup salt
1 tablespoon cream of tartar (do NOT omit this)
2 tablespoons cooking oil

CAUTION: To be prepared by an adult only, as a stove is involved.

Pour dry ingredients in a large pan and mix well. Add water and oil and stir well over medium heat with a wooden spoon until mixture pulls together. Remove from heat. Knead well and store in airtight container or large plastic bag.

D. WHAT'S SO AMAZING ABOUT OCTOPUSES? (10–15 minutes)

Purpose

To introduce children to some of the fascinating features of this eight-armed creature

Materials

(for each child)

- plastic cup (CAUTION: Do not allow children to put cups over their noses and mouths.)
- masking tape
- scotch tape
- paper (can be copy paper, tissue paper, or construction paper)
- scissors
- measuring cup (¼ or ½)
- googly eyes or paper
- tacky glue
- red paper
- hole protectors or circles cut with a hole punch
- suction cups

- balloons (larger balloons are easier to blow up)
- outline of octopus, drawn on paper and copied for each child
- gray, brown, and black crayons or gray, brown, and black pieces of paper
- rock (optional)
- school glue
- clear plastic cup
- dry erase marker
- blue or black food dye
- sink or pitcher of water

Note: As with the hummingbird activity, the different Fact/Act pairs can be set up as separate stations. One option is to spread the Fact information and Act materials along a long table, buffet style. Children can start at one end of the table and move down the line, adding on to their octopus model as they go.

Procedure

First, read a fact (Fact) to the children and explain if necessary, then follow with the activity (Act). The first few Facts and Acts will build a simple model of the octopus.

FACT: The body of the octopus is a bulging head and eight arms. It doesn't have a skeleton or shell, so it is really squishy.
ACT: Use a plastic cup for the octopus's head. Then cut eight strips of paper and tape them to the open end of the cup.

FACT: The octopus has large eyes that can see clearly in dark or cloudy water. Because it has these great eyes, the octopus can hunt at night.
ACT: Attach two googly eyes to the head of the octopus, using the tacky glue. (Alternate eyes: Cut two circles from paper and glue them to the head.)

FACT: How many hearts do you have? (Allow time for response.) An octopus has three hearts!
ACT: Cut three hearts from the red paper (any shape will do) and glue them to the head of the octopus.

FACT: Put a piece of candy on your arm. Say: "Yum. That candy tastes good!" When the children protest, ask them how they taste candy. Tell them that although we can't taste with our arms, an octopus does! The arms of the octopus are covered with suction cups that let the octopus taste what it's touching!

ACT: Put "suction cups" on the arms of your octopus by sticking the hole protectors up and down one side of each arm. (Alternate: Glue hole-punched circles to the arms of your octopus.)

FACT: The suction cups on the octopus's arms are not just for tasting; they help the octopus move by clinging to surfaces, like the ocean floor and rocks.

ACT: Give children suction cups and let them experiment by sticking them to surfaces and pulling them off.

FACT: When an octopus moves with its suction cups, it doesn't go super fast. If it needs to get away in a hurry, it does something else. (Blow up balloon, but don't let it go.) Say, "The octopus fills its body with water, the way I filled this balloon with air." (Let go of the balloon.) "When the octopus shoots the water out one way, its body shoots very quickly the other way. This helps the octopus escape from enemies."

ACT: Let children blow up balloons and let them go. Help them see that the air comes out one end of the balloon and the balloon shoots in the opposite direction.

Note: For health reasons, do not allow children to share balloons.

FACT: Other animals, such as sharks, eels, and dolphins, like to eat octopuses. The octopus doesn't have a hard shell to protect it, but it has other ways of keeping safe. The first way is to change the way it looks. The octopus can change its color and even texture to blend in to its surroundings. In other words, it can make itself look like a rock!

ACT: Give each child the outline of the octopus and the gray, brown, and black crayons. Have the child color the octopus to look like a rock. If you want, you can provide a rock sample for the child to look at. (Alternate: Instead of using crayons, let the child tear black, brown, and gray paper into small pieces and glue them in the octopus outline.)

FACT: If an octopus is spotted by an animal that wants to eat it, the octopus can release a cloud of black ink that hides the octopus and gives it time to get away.

ACT: Give one child a clear plastic cup and dry erase marker. Let the child draw a small octopus on the outside of the cup. Then fill the cup with water and have the child look through the cup, with the octopus on the opposite side of the child. Squeeze a few drops of food coloring into the water. The octopus will disappear.

Note: To minimize waste, erase the octopus after the child has done the activity and reuse the cup with other children. The cups can be cleaned or recycled at the end of the activity.

E. PHOTO SAFARI (15–30 minutes, or as long as desired)

It's time to get the kids into nature. Divide kids into small groups, with one adult and one digital camera per group. Let the kids take a nature walk and photograph things that inspire them. You might give them some directions, like trying to find one thing smaller than your thumb or finding a group of three things, and so on, so you don't wind up with forty pictures of trees. Have photos made to be put together in a collage for the next night. If digital cameras are not available, you can use disposable, but you can't erase blurry or unusable shots or pick and choose your pictures. If cameras are not an option, give kids paper and colored pencils and let them draw what they see.

F. HOW TO BUILD AN EAGLE NEST (10–15 minutes, or as long as desired)

Note: This activity requires substantial preparation, but it's great fun for the children and a good activity for children who need to move. The instructions are specific, but feel free to improvise. After all, no two eagle nests look alike.

Materials

- newspapers (You will need a lot!)
- pencils
- masking tape (at least 2 rolls)
- ½-inch PVC pipes (lengths below)
- PVC cement
- PVC purple primer
- ten PVC couplings for ½-inch pipe
- eight PVC 45-degree elbows for ½-inch pipe
- ten PVC tees for ½-inch pipe
- book with pictures of an eagle's nest

Note on PVC lengths: You will need approximately forty feet of PVC pipe, cut into the following lengths:

- 2 feet x 5
- 3 feet x 5
- 20 inches x 2
- 15¾ inches x 4
- 15 inches x 4
- 1 inch x 8

You will need only a small amount of primer and cement, so ask if someone has some you can use.

Advanced Preparation

There are two stages to the preparation: one to roll newspaper for "sticks" and the other to build a base for the nest.

Newspaper Branches: Enlist helpers to speed this step along. For each newspaper stick, you will need three double sheets of newspaper. Open the newspapers and stack the sheets on top of each other. Lay the pencil at one corner and start rolling the newspaper over it. Once you get the roll going, pull the pencil out. Roll to the opposite corner and secure with tape. The more tightly you can roll the newspaper, the better it will hold up during the nest building. Roll 150 to 200 sticks.

Nest Base: CAUTION: Carefully follow the instructions for the PVC primer and cement. Do not use indoors or around children.

If you are using an electric saw to cut the pipes, be sure to wear protective goggles and follow manufacturer's instructions. Do not allow children to cut pipes or stand near the saw. Remember, cut edges may be sharp.

1. Cut the pipes to the lengths specified, or to the lengths you have determined for your own design.
2. Lay the pipes, elbows, and tees on the ground in this order to form an elongated octagon (inch measurement given denotes the pipe of that length): 20 inch, tee, 1 inch,

elbow, 15 inch, tee, 1 inch, elbow, 15¾ inch, tee, 15¾ inch, elbow, 1 inch, tee, 15 inch, elbow, 1 inch, tee, 20 inch, tee, 1 inch, elbow, 15 inch, tee, 1 inch, elbow, 15¾ inch, tee, 15¾ inch, elbow, 1 inch tee, 15 inch, elbow, 1 inch, tee.

3. Using the PVC purple primer and cement and following the manufacturer's instructions, prime and glue the pieces together. The tees should point slightly outward. *Note:* If you will need to transport the base to another location, consider how large your vehicle is. You may need to glue the base in sections and glue the sections together once you have transported it.

4. After the cement has dried, the 2-foot and 3-foot pipes will be inserted into the tees to form branches. Remember to prime and cement the pipes. Cover the exposed ends of these pipes with the couplings to protect children's hands. If you choose, leave one of the pipes out, to create a larger opening for children to enter the nest.

Procedure

If the children built a hummingbird nest, ask them how large it was. Say, "Some hummingbirds build nests that are less than an inch long. Some birds, though, build really large nests. The bald eagle builds the largest tree nest, sometimes as long as eight or nine feet, though most bald eagle nests are about five to six feet long."

Show the children pictures of a bald eagle nest and point out how sticks are woven between branches. Then show the children the newspaper sticks and the PVC base. Tell them the base is like the branches of the tree and the newspaper is like the sticks the eagles bring back to weave in the branches. Tell them they will build a nest by taping the sticks to the branches.

Enlist a couple of helpers to tear off pieces of tape to hand to children, so they can tape the sticks to the branches. Don't worry about how the nest looks. The big idea is for children to grasp how large the nest is.

Summary and Closing (10–15 minutes)

Materials

- "This Is My Father's World" photo slideshow and music downloaded from YouTube (kids' version http://www.youtube.com/watch?v=roLmIXlpPc8)

Debriefing in Small Groups (10 minutes)

Generate discussion with the following questions:

1. What was your favorite activity that you did today?

2. Why did you like this activity so much?

3. What is something that you learned today?

4. How do you now feel about God's creation after learning so much about it today?

5. How did learning about creation make you feel about God?

6. God's creation is pretty amazing, huh? Why do you think God made such fascinating creatures like the blue whale, polar bear, hummingbird, and octopus? Why do you think God's creatures have so much detail?

7. What is a way you want to continue to look at creation or nature when you get home?

Tying It All Together

Play the video "This Is My Father's World" as a closing, meditative focal piece that will leave the children with a positive feeling.

CLOSING PRAYER

O God, Maker of all that is seen in this wide, wonderful universe that is our home: Open our eyes to the beauty of the world around us. Help us to take time to see, to listen, to touch, to taste, and to smell the blessings that have been created. And may we join all creation in singing forth praise. Amen.

TWO

Respect for God's Creation

SCRIPTURE TEXTS
Psalm 24:1–2; Psalm 8

THEME OF THE DAY
Respecting creation

VERSE OF THE DAY
The earth is the Lord's. (Psalm 24:1)

PURPOSE OF THE LESSON
*To help children gain a respect for the interdependent web
of all creation of which each of us is a part and learn that the
earth is not ours to do with as we please.*

FOR THE LEADER—AN OPENING MEDITATION

In the ancient psalmist's understanding, "the earth is the Lord's." In other words, all creation belongs to the great Giver of Life. Yet, at the same time, human beings play a vital role in caring for the great web of life of which we also are a part. What we are learning is the earth is not ours to do with as we please. "Dominion" over the earth, as the traditional versions of the Bible translate it in the opening creation story (Genesis 1:26) and Psalm 8, does not mean doing with the earth and its resources as we please. Dominion theology is being reinterpreted as a theology of respect, with the understanding that humankind is not above but intricately related to and dependent upon all creation.

Contemporary writer Sue Monk Kidd speaks of what she calls a "We-consciousness." Kidd contends, "Humans, having special abilities, are responsible to the rest of the earth, not superior to it. We will realize that everything here has a purpose all its own, that its value lies in its own 'beingness,' not in its usefulness or how well it benefits humankind. This means something dramatically new—that the rest of creation is here to be related to, not dominated" (Kidd, *The Dance of the Dissident Daughter*, 1996, 162).

As the Native Americans have long understood, we cannot own the earth. We are just passing through this life and are privileged to share in the beauty and bounty of the earth for a time. All creation is to be shared with others and kept in trust for those who will come after us. "This we know—the earth does not belong to us, we belong to the earth" is the way that Chief Seattle put it. Simply put, we need to learn, as the Lakota Sioux say, "to live well in the natural world."

Many of us still have much to learn about respecting this wonderful earth that we call home. So let's get started on our adventure of learning new ways of living in relationship with God's amazing creation!

GATHERING TIME

Purpose

To provide an example of disrespect toward the earth that will begin children's dialoguing about the consequences

Gathering Music

"For the Beauty of the Earth" (*New Century Hymnal*, #28) or another familiar hymn

Materials

- two or three cardboard or wooden tree props
- tempera or acrylic paint for painting props
- a trash can full of trash
- stuffed or cardboard squirrels, birds, butterflies, bees, hummingbirds on sticks (to be held by children)
- a "flowerbed" made with satin or paper flowers

- a beach ball or kickball
- foam "rocks"
- nature posters (including posters showing both the beauty of the earth and pollution and destruction of the earth)
- large sheet of paper
- marker
- CD player
- CD with Gathering Music
- masking tape

Advance Preparations

1. Hang the posters around the room for the students to look at throughout the day. But wait until the end of the lesson to discuss them.

2. Write the verse of the day on a large sheet of paper and hang.

3. Select children to rehearse and present the following skit. Set the stage for the skit.

4. Provide seating, as for Lesson One.

GETTING STARTED (5–10 minutes)

Play the music softly in the background, as children arrive.

Say, "Now we are going to watch a short skit. As we do, be thinking about how the actions of those in the skit make you feel and what you might do if you were to see something like this happen in real life."

Opening Scene: A boy and girl are playing ball in the park

BOY: Hey sis, let's see how far apart we can throw the ball.

GIRL: Ok. Hey, I'm glad we came to the park today. It's so nice here.

The boy and girl continue throwing the ball as a couple of rowdy kids walk up and begin vandalizing the park: trampling the flower beds, throwing down trash, throwing rocks at squirrels and birds. When the unruly kids trample the flowers, the bees, birds, and hummingbirds fly away (children holding these exit). When they throw "rocks" at squirrels, they run away.

BOY: Can you believe what they are doing?

GIRL: No! That's bad!

BOY: What should we do?

GIRL: I don't know. I'm kind of scared. Maybe we should go home.

BOY: Don't you think we should do something? They're ruining the park!

GIRL: What can we do? They are a lot bigger than us.

BOY: I guess you're right. Let's go. I don't like it here any more.

The boy and girl leave to go home.

SHARING TIME

(Children may be divided into small groups.)

Materials

- book: *The Wolves Are Back*, by Jean Craighead George
- the following words and/or pictures on separate pieces of paper to accompany the book: wolf, raven, golden eagle, grizzly bear, magpie, mouse, beetle, deer, elk, antelope, sparrow, flycatcher, bison, grass, aspen, willows, beaver, water birds, fish, frogs, dragonflies, coyotes, ground squirrels, badgers, wildflowers, mountain sheep, bees, butterflies, warblers, hummingbirds
- U.S. map showing Yellowstone National Park
- book: *John Muir: America's Naturalist*, by Thomas Locker
- book: *America's National Parks*, Crescent Books
- Bibles
- copies of questions
- pens
- big piece of white paper, taped to the wall
- markers
- books on ecology, nature, animals, ecosystems, pollution
- nature boxes (see "Make a Display" under C. below)
- drawing paper and colored pencils

A. DISCOVERING CONTEMPORARY IDEAS ABOUT RESPECT FOR CREATION

Sharing My Life (5–10 minutes)

Purpose

To give children the opportunity to discuss the skit and reflect on repercussions of irresponsible actions

Opening Small Group Questions

1. What happened in the skit?

2. Why do you think the trouble-making kids acted like that?

3. What happened to the insects and animals? (They left.)

4. How did it make you feel when the kids trampled the flowers, hurt the animals, and tossed trash on the ground?

5. Why do you think you felt that way?

6. Could the boy and girl have done something about it? If so, what? (Possible responses include running to get an adult to help, calling the police, waiting until the kids were gone and picking up the trash. It is important to explain to the children that they should not confront the older kids, as this could put them in danger).

7. Look at the long-term picture of what might happen because of what these kids did. (Possibilities: Without the flowers, the bees, butterflies, and hummingbirds might not return. People might be afraid to play there. Help children start to understand that actions can have greater effects than they realize.)

8. How can the problems be fixed? (Flowers could be replanted so the birds and insects would return, trash can be cleaned up, and so on. Begin to formulate the idea that humans need to fix what we and others have messed up.)

9. Have you ever seen someone not showing respect for or doing something bad to the earth?

10. Can you think of something you might have done in that situation to help fix it?

Sharing Others' Experiences of Respect for Creation (15–30 minutes)

Note: Choose either *The Wolves Are Back* or *John Muir* from the "Materials" list. Lesson plans follow for each.

Book One: *The Wolves Are Back*

Purpose

Humans need to look at the big picture of how their actions affect the delicate ecosystems of creation.

Procedure

Say, "In our skit, the kids who destroyed the flowers probably didn't think about the birds and the bees and the butterflies' leaving. Our skit was make-believe. Now we are going to read about a time when people destroyed wolves and a lot of other things happened that the people didn't think about."

Read the book.

Help children find Yellowstone National Park on the map.

Say, "The Lamar Valley in Yellowstone National Park had a lot of different kinds of plants and animals in it." (Lay the cards with animal words or pictures on the floor, naming each one.) "Then some people decided that there shouldn't be any wolves."

"Why do you think people thought this?" (Take the wolf card out of the group and put aside.)

"But when the wolves were killed off, a lot more changed that people didn't expect." (Remove the cards for sparrow, flycatcher, aspens, grass, willows, beaver, water birds, fish, frogs, dragonfly, ground squirrels, wildflowers, bees, butterflies, warblers, and hummingbirds.)

"Why do you think all these things disappeared?" (You can help children recall information from the book or they can come up with their own ideas. The big idea is that everything is connected and removing one part affects the whole.)

"People didn't mean for all this to happen, so they wanted to fix it. What did they do?" (They reintroduced the wolves.) "What happened when the wolves returned?" (The other species returned/thrived.)

Book Two: *John Muir: America's Naturalist*

Purpose

To introduce the idea that the earth isn't ours to do with as we please

Procedure

Say, "In our skit, the kids who destroyed the flowers may have thought that it was okay for them to do whatever they liked to the earth. Now we are going to read a book about a man who loved nature and thought we should respect it."

Read the book. Tell the children that in John Muir's day, people thought they could do what they wanted with the earth. Ask, "Did John Muir think this?" (No, he believed that human are not the masters of nature.)

Ask the group what John Muir did to help protect and respect nature. (He helped create the national park system.)

Show photos of national parks.

B. DISCOVERING A BIBLICAL VIEW ABOUT RESPECT FOR CREATION (15–30 minutes)

Tell the group, "People are starting to learn that we can't just do what we want with the earth. Let's read some Bible verses and see if we can get some ideas for how humans should live in the world." Explain to your group how to find the book of Psalms and how to turn to the chapters and verses (open to the middle of the Bible or look in the table of contents). Read Psalm 24:1–2 as a group.

Questions for Discussion

1. What are these verses about?

2. Why do you think the writer wrote these verses?

3. What do these verses say about the earth and everything that is in it?

4. To whom does the earth belong?

Read Psalm 8 as a group; then discuss the following questions:

1. What kind of relationship do you think God wants to have with people? (A close and caring one)

2. What kind of model does God set for us and how we relate with others and all creatures of the earth? (A good model, respect, and like answers)

3. What do you think Psalm 8:6 means, and how do you think God meant for everyone to treat the earth and everyone and everything in it when it was entrusted to our care? (Caring for and sharing the earth's resources with all creation)

4. How should you treat something that does not belong to you?

5. What does it mean to respect something? (Tell the group that a lot of times when you respect something, you learn more about it. If we want to learn how to respect God's creation more, we need to learn more about creation.)

6. Does this give you ideas for how we should treat the earth?

7. What is one aspect of God's creation your group wants to learn more about? (It could be a certain type of animal or plant, how pollution affects the earth, a certain continent, bodies of water, or anything about the earth and living things.)

Allow about ten to fifteen minutes for group study and discussion. Then call the large group back together. Go through the questions one at a time, allowing each group to share some of their group's answers. For question #7, have a large sheet of blank paper on the wall entitled "Learning More about Earth." Ask each group to send someone to come up and write the group's idea to question #7 on the wall. Go over all the answers with the group.

C. ENCOURAGING CHILDREN'S CREATIVITY (15–30 minutes)

Learning through Drawing

Instruct the students to look at their answers to #7 in the preceding questions. Ask them to choose one aspect of creation to learn more about when they go home (they can choose a different aspect from their group's answer or one that is not even listed). Pass out pieces of drawing paper and colored pencils. Instruct the students to draw a picture of their choice. When students are finished, ask them to return to their small groups and share their drawings. Suggest that the students ask their parents to take them to the library to check out books and videos on their aspect of creation.

Learning through Reading

Make available many books on ecology, different ecosystems, animals, plants, the effects of pollution, and so on, for students to look through as their interests lead them during breaks between activities.

Make a Display

Make a display of several different boxes with objects from nature for the students to study (leaves, plants, insects, small animals). Provide magnifying glasses to entice children to look at the display.

ACTIVITY TIME

A. MAKE A MODEL GATOR (10–15 minutes)

Purpose

Children will make alligators as a reminder of what they learned from the book *Who Lives in an Alligator Hole?*

Materials

- *Who Lives in an Alligator Hole?* by Anne Rockwell
- miniature marshmallows (CAUTION: Do not allow children to stuff marshmallows into their mouths, as this may obstruct breathing.)
- craft glue, such as Tacky glue
- sheets of paper or wax paper
- green and black paint
- paintbrushes
- three-ounce paper cups
- picture of alligator

FUN FACT: IN THE UNITED STATES, A YEAR'S WORTH OF ALUMINUM CANS THAT ARE THROWN IN THE TRASH WOULD PROVIDE ENOUGH ALUMINUM TO MAKE MORE THAN EIGHT THOUSAND 747 AIRPLANES.

Procedure

Read *Who Lives in an Alligator Hole?* and give children a chance to talk about it. If time is short, or if children are tired of listening, summarize the book in your own words, while showing the pictures. Or, if you prefer, read and discuss the book while the children are making their models.

Give each child a sheet of paper or wax paper and a handful of marshmallows.

Squeeze a spot of glue at one corner of each child's paper. Children can dab marshmallows in the glue and stick them together to build a model alligator on their paper.

Once a child is satisfied with his or her model, give him or her a three-ounce cup with a little green paint and a paintbrush to paint the model. Black paint can be used to add eyes.

Allow the model to dry overnight. In the meantime, children can make a model alligator hole. (See next activity.)

B. MAKE A MODEL ALLIGATOR HOLE (10–15 minutes)

Purpose

To reinforce the lesson in *Who Lives in an Alligator Hole?* by building a model hole for the marshmallow alligator

Materials

- homemade play dough (find the recipe on page 24)
- brown paint
- paintbrushes
- three-ounce paper cups
- cardboard from old food/cereal boxes

Procedure

Give each child a piece of cardboard and a handful of play dough. If you are using food boxes, make sure the plain side is up because it will be easier to paint.

Children should pat the dough out. Don't let them make it too thin or there won't be enough depth to make a hole. Have children use their fists to make an indention in the center of the clay. Remind them that the alligator swishes its head and tail to make a hole and they can swish their fists back and forth. The hole should be long and wide enough for their alligator to fit in.

When the play dough is dry (overnight), give each child a little brown paint in a three-ounce paper cup and let him or her paint the model. Once the paint has dried, the marshmallow alligator can be added.

C. MODEL WETLAND (10–15 minutes)

Purpose

Wetlands benefit nature and humans. This model will help children understand how important wetlands are.

Materials

- shallow pans
- cereal boxes
- wax paper
- tape
- sponges
- cups
- water
- bucket
- book with pictures of wetlands and animals that inhabit them

Advanced Preparation

1. Cut one side of the cereal box and trim to the width of the sponge.
2. Cover this cardboard with wax paper and tape to the back.
3. Repeat until you have enough for a small group, with children working in pairs.

Procedure

If the children have not heard *Who Lives in an Alligator Hole?* consider sharing this before you begin the activity.

Pair the children up and give each pair a prepared cardboard, sponge, and cup of water. Say, "Today you heard the book *Who Lives in an Alligator Hole?* Alligators live in a special kind of place, called a wetland. Wetlands are important because they are home to lots of animals." (Show pictures from the wetland book.) "Wetlands are also important because they keep rivers from flooding."

Instruct one child in each pair to put one end of the cardboard in the pan and hold it at a gentle slope. Then take the sponge and lay it so it reaches all the way across the cardboard, about halfway down. The sponge is the wetland and the pan is the river. Say, "The cup of water you have is the rain. Let's see what happens to the rain when we have a wetland." They should slowly pour the water at the high end of the cardboard. Some of the water will run into the pan, but most of it will be caught by the wetland.

Dialogue with the children about where the water went. Tell them that one of the important benefits of wetlands is catching rainwater so that it doesn't cause the river to overflow and flood the land. Instruct them to squeeze the water from the sponge into the bucket, then set the sponge aside.

Give each pair more water. Tell children that sometimes people drain wetlands so that they can build on them. Instruct children to slowly pour the rain on the cardboard, like before, but without the sponge. All the water flows to the river.

Talk again with the children about what happened. Without the wetland, water drains to the river, which can cause the river to overflow its banks. Walk around with the bucket and collect water.

Tell the children, "Now we know two things that wetlands are good for: as habitats and to prevent flooding."

D. WEAVE A TANGLED WEB (15–30 minutes)

Purpose

To provide a visual example of how intricately related members of an ecosystem are

Materials

- index cards
- tape
- marker

- yarn
- scissors

Advanced Preparation

Write the following words on the index cards: sun, tree, grass, flower, berries, moose, mosquito, fungus, butterfly, bee, caterpillar, vole, bird, squirrel, bear, fox.

Note: There are a lot of connections in this web. If children get restless before the end, stop. They will be tangled enough to understand the point.

Procedure

You will need sixteen to twenty children for this activity. Tape the index cards to sixteen children. If you have more children, they can help with the next steps.

Cut four lengths of yarn, about a yard each, and connect the sun to the grass, the flower, the berries, and the tree. (In other words, give all four pieces of yarn to the sun to hold. Give the other end of one piece to the grass, another to the flower, another to the berries, and the last to the tree.) Tell children that plants need sun to grow. *Note:* As the web gets more tangled, you'll have to cut longer lengths of yarn.

Cut four lengths of yarn and connect the grass to the vole, the caterpillar, the bird, and the fox. Tell the children that all these animals eat the grass.

Cut five lengths and connect the berries to the bear, the squirrel, the bird, the fox, and the vole. Tell the children that all these animals eat the berries.

Cut five lengths and connect the flower to the bird, the butterfly, the bee, the mosquito, and the vole. Tell the children that these animals drink nectar from the flower or eat seeds that grow from the flower.

Cut six lengths and connect the tree to the moose, the fungus, the squirrel, the bird, the vole, and the fox. The tree provides food through its bark, its leaves, and nuts. The tree is also home to animals.

Cut two lengths and connect the fungus to the vole and the squirrel. There are many types of fungi, and some are food for these animals.

Cut two lengths and connect the vole to the bear and the fox. Voles are small animals that are eaten by some larger animals.

Cut three lengths and connect the moose to the bear, the vole, and the mosquito. The mosquito can drink the moose's blood; the vole might nibble on a dead moose's antler. And the bear might eat the moose.

Cut three lengths and connect the bird to the mosquito, the caterpillar, and the fox. The bird might eat the mosquito and the caterpillar. The fox will be especially hungry for bird eggs.

Cut two lengths and connect the fox to the squirrel and the caterpillar. The fox might eat these animals.

Cut two lengths and connect the squirrel to the bird and the caterpillar. A squirrel might eat a bird egg and the caterpillar.

Give children the opportunity to talk about the web.

E. LEARNING TO SEE THE BIG PICTURE (10–15 minutes)

Purpose

To help children grasp the concept that when we look only at one part, we don't see the whole picture

Materials

- Books with cutouts, such as *Banana Moon* by Janet Marshall or *Shark in the Park* by Nick Sharratt

Procedure

Read the book. As you turn to a page with a window that reveals part of the next page, dialogue with the children about what the object looks like. If you prefer, don't read the text, but simply show children the partially hidden objects and let them guess what they are. When you turn the page to reveal the full picture, ask children how their ideas changed once they saw everything.

Discuss with children how this is similar to what happened to the wolves in Yellowstone and to alligators. When people looked only at one animal, they failed to see the whole picture of how that animal was connected to everything else. When we don't see the whole picture, we can harm nature without meaning to.

F. FOLLOW-UP TO "LEARNING TO SEE THE BIG PICTURE" (10–15 minutes)

Purpose

To make a partially revealed picture, to reinforce the importance of looking at the big picture.

Materials

- construction paper
- copy paper
- crayons
- scissors
- tape

Advanced Preparation

1. Photo copy or print out a variety of coloring pages.
2. Cut one small window in each sheet of construction paper. Vary the placement of windows.

Procedure, Option One (for younger children)

Let each child choose a coloring page and color it.

Next let each child choose a sheet of construction paper to place over the coloring page. Children may want to try different pages to see which suits their picture best. Once a piece of construction paper has been selected, the child should place it on top of the coloring page and tape all along one side.

With the construction paper covering the coloring page, let the child imagine what the partially revealed picture looks like. He or she can write this on the top sheet.

Encourage children to share their pictures with family and friends to see if they are surprised by what the whole picture is.

Procedure, Option Two (for older children)

Explain to the children that they are going to make pictures similar to those in *Banana Moon* or *Shark in the Park*, with one page covering most of the picture on a second page.

Pass out supplies and let the children design their own pictures and cut their own windows. Have them place the construction page, with the window, on top of the colored page and tape all along one side.

Encourage children to share their pictures with family and friends, to see if they are surprised by what the whole picture is.

G. INVITE A NATURE SPECIALIST

Invite a local ecologist or a nature preserve or wildlife ranger to come and give a talk or demonstration on how all of nature is interconnected.

H. PLAN A TRIP

Take a group trip (perhaps at the end of the day) to a nature observatory or park to observe nature. While there, provide paper and pens for any students who might like to write a short reflection or prayer of praise for God's marvelous creation.

SUMMARY AND CLOSING (10–15 minutes)

Debriefing in Small Groups

Use the following questions to guide discussion:

1. What was your favorite activity that you did today?

2. Why did you like this activity so much?

3. How do you think the crafts we made and the things we talked about are connected?

4. What is something that you learned today?

5. In what ways can you know God better by discovering so much about creation?

Tying It All Together: Discuss the following questions about the nature posters hanging on the walls around the room:

1. Do any of the posters on the wall stand out to you? Why?

2. How does seeing the different posters make you feel after learning about the sacredness, fragility, and complexity of nature today?

3. Do you feel you are starting to have a greater respect for both God and creation? How so?

4. What is one way you will think differently about nature from now on?

CLOSING PRAYER (a prayer inspired by the Ojibway of North America)

God of creation: in many ways our world is broken. People have not always done what they should have done to care for the earth. All of us must learn how to better care for our world. So teach us love and compassion so we may respect and help heal the earth. Amen.

THREE

Keepers of God's Creation

SCRIPTURE TEXTS
Genesis 2:8–9, 15

THEME OF THE DAY
Becoming responsible "keepers" of the earth

VERSE OF THE DAY
God put the man and woman in the garden to keep it. (Genesis 2:15)

PURPOSE OF THE LESSON
To encourage children (and their families) to care
for the earth by recycling and reusing its resources and by
replacing inefficient items.

FOR THE LEADER—AN OPENING MEDITATION

If we were to grade ourselves on how well we have been "keepers" of the earth, how would we fare? Would we receive a passing grade? Many of us might have to answer that we have not fared well. One need only drive through the rural countryside and see the scores of junk car graveyards, or visit our lakes and oceans that are sometimes so polluted it is not safe to get in the water, or visit one of our city or county landfills to realize that we have missed the mark. We have become a "throw away" society. We have grown accustomed to and comfortable with throwing away practically everything—old automobiles, plastic bags and bottles, old television sets, microwaves. You name it, and we probably throw it away. And all our throwaways have polluted God's good earth.

When the writer of the ancient book of Genesis spoke of humankind being commissioned to till the earth and keep it, the writer had no concept of recycling in the modern sense. But today we know that a responsible keeping of the earth has to include the practice of recycling, as well as replacing high-energy-consuming items with more efficient ones.

Perhaps the hope of our earth's future lies with our children who catch the vision of a renewed earth.

So let's get started thinking about practical ways that all of us can become more responsible keepers of the earth by recycling, reusing, and replacing!

GATHERING TIME

Purpose

To introduce the concepts of recycling and reusing by using discards to create something new

Gathering Music

"How Beautiful, Our Spacious Skies" (*New Century Hymnal*, #594) or another familiar hymn

Materials

- yogurt cups
- cereal boxes
- milk cartons, plastic and cardboard
- lids and caps
- mesh baskets, such as hold berries
- small scraps of wood
- material scraps
- scissors
- glue

- hammer
- nails
- goggles
- large sheet of paper
- marker
- CD player
- CD with Gathering Music

Advanced Preparations

1. Write the verse of the day on a large sheet of paper and hang.

2. Provide seating, as for Lesson One.

3. Assemble the materials on a table. Solicit volunteers to assist children with hammering.

GETTING STARTED (10–15 minutes)

Play the music softly in the background. As children arrive, instruct them to use the materials and their imagination to build something. CAUTION: If children hammer, make sure they and assisting adults are wearing goggles.

Note: If you prefer, rather than an open-ended activity, you can instruct the children to make specific items, such as drums from oatmeal boxes or guitars from tissue boxes and rubber bands. A simple car can be made by hammering four milk cap wheels onto a scrap block of wood.

SHARING TIME

(Children may be divided into small groups if you have more than one copy of the book.)

Materials

- *Something from Nothing* by Phoebe Gilman
- alternate book, *Joseph Had a Little Overcoat,* by Simms Taback
- Bibles
- copies of questions

A. DISCOVERING CONTEMPORARY EXPERIENCES OF KEEPING CREATION BY REUSING AND RECYCLING

Sharing My Life (5–10 minutes)

Purpose

To begin thinking about what it means to be responsible for something

Opening Small Group Questions

1. Have you ever helped take care of something, like a younger brother or sister, a pet, a plant, or a library book?

2. What did you need to do in order to take good care of it? (brother or sister—bottle, diapers, rattle, etc.; pet——feed it, walk it, give it a bath, play with it, love it; plant—water it, give it sunlight; book—make sure it did not get lost or damaged)

3. How did it make you feel having the responsibility of caring for it?

Sharing Others' Experiences of Keeping Creation by Reusing and Recycling (15–30 minutes)

Purpose

To explore the idea of being responsible by reusing and recycling things instead of throwing them away

Procedure

Say to the group, "When you came today, there was a pile of trash on the table. Instead of throwing it away, you made something new from it. Now, we are going to read a story about a grandfather who was very creative in reusing things."

Read the book *Something from Nothing* by Phoebe Gilman or *Joseph Had a Little Overcoat* by Simms Taback.

Questions for Discussion

1. At the beginning of the book, what was the new thing the grandfather made?

2. How many times did he reuse that thing to make something new? I was very impressed with his imagination. How about you?

3. Can you think of something that you have that has been recycled from something else? (recycled paper, plastic containers, plastic benches, cloth bags) *Note:* The website http://www.recycledproducts.com/ has many recycled products.

4. Can you think of something you have now that could be remade into something new? (examples: an old pair of jeans could be made into shorts or a bag; an old t-shirt can be used as a cleaning rag, sewn to make a shopping bag, or cut into strips to make a rag rug; birthday or greeting cards can be cut and made into bookmarks; pictures from magazines or old cards can be cut out to make new greeting cards, etc.)

5. Why is it important to reuse and recycle things that are important to us? (We are able to use fewer new products. We can keep the sentimental item longer.)

B. DISCOVERING A BIBLICAL VIEW OF KEEPING CREATION (15–30 minutes)

Say, "The person who wrote the book of Genesis believed that when God created the earth and people, humans were given the job of taking care of the earth. Let's take a look at these verses and talk about how we might take care of the earth."

Explain to your group how to find the book of Genesis and how to turn to the chapter and verses. Read Genesis 2:8–9, 15 as a group.

Questions for Discussion

1. Imagine that we could jump into this story. How do you think the garden would look? What words might describe the garden? (perfect, beautiful, clean, new, pure, natural, unpolluted)

2. Why do you think God made such beautiful and wonderful things in creation?

3. How does that garden compare with the earth now?

4. Verse 15: What do you think it means that God put humans in charge of "working and taking care of" the garden? Why do you think God wants us to take good care of the earth? (so we have good things to enjoy, eat, see, and so on) Tell the children that God loves us very much and wants us to have good things on the earth and also wants us to take good care of them.

5. What kinds of things can we do to help take care of the earth?

6. One way we can help take care of the earth is to use less energy. Can you think of some things you can do at home to help cut down on how much energy you consume every day? (Examples include turning off the water when brushing teeth or washing hands, taking shorter showers, turning off lights when you leave a room, shutting

doors when you go outside to keep the air conditioning or heat in, rewearing clothes another day if they are not dirty.)

7. Two more ways we can help take care of the earth is to recycle and reuse items more. Can you think of some things you can do at home to recycle or reuse more? (Examples include using reusable drinking bottles instead of disposable plastic water bottles or juice boxes; using both sides of paper for homework, coloring, or drawing; throwing aluminum cans and plastic bottles in recycling instead of the trash can.)

C. ENCOURAGING CHILDREN'S CREATIVITY (15–30 minutes)

Learn about Energy Consumption

Set up a table with examples of high-energy-consuming products paired with energy efficient products. Talk about how important it is to replace the energy-consuming items. Use the following list and add your own ideas:

incandescent bulb vs. compact fluorescent light bulb

conventional battery vs. rechargeable battery

photo of a clothes dryer vs. drying rack or clothes pins

plastic/paper grocery bags vs. reusable fabric bags

power strips for items that stay plugged in, to reduce power usage

CAUTION: Keep bulbs in packaging to reduce risk of injury from breakage, and do not allow children to plug in power strips.

Learn about Recycling

Set up a table with items that can and cannot be recycled. Set a recycle bin and trash can on the floor. Pick up an item with the recycle symbol and show it to the children. Explain that this symbol means the item can be recycled and should go in the recycle bin. Let the children explore all the items, looking for the recycle symbol. Ask the children to sort recyclable items into the recycle bin and those that cannot be recycled into a trash can. Talk about the importance of buying recycled and recyclable items.

Note: Check with your community to find out what items are recyclable where you live, including what numbers are accepted.

Generally Recyclable Items

- plastic water bottles
- shampoo bottles
- plastic milk containers
- any plastic container with the recycling symbol and #
- aluminum cans
- glass containers
- paper (newspaper, magazines, envelopes, used paper, office paper)
- cardboard
- some styrofoam (check for recycling symbol and #)

Some Things Not Recyclable

- paper container with food on it
- plastic containers and items without the recycling symbol and #
- aluminum foil and pie pans

ACTIVITY TIME

For all kinds of fun tips and activities, visit the online resource http://greenguidefor kids.blogspot.com.

A. GARBAGE ARCHEOLOGY (15–30 minutes)

Purpose

In this activity, children will do an archeological dig of garbage to learn how much we throw away of different items. This activity also sets the stage for the later lesson on reducing garbage.

Materials

- paper products—newspaper, junk mail, and packaging
- metals—soda cans (CAUTION: Do not use cans that have sharp edges, such as steel food cans.)

- glass substitute—plastic containers with lids (see note)
- artificial plants
- food substitute—pictures of foods glued to cardboard
- plastic—especially plastics used for packaging (CAUTION: Do not include anything that has been in contract with raw meat.)
- plastic shopping bags (CAUTION: Do not allow children to put bags over their faces, as suffocation could occur.)
- wood—such as craft sticks (CAUTION: Do not use wood with splintered edges.)
- sand
- duct tape
- eight boxes for sorting trash items
- eight index cards
- marker
- large container for garbage pile
- calculator

Note: To make a substitute for glass, determine how heavy the glass should be. Add sand to a plastic container until it is the correct weight and tape the lid on with the duct tape. Label this as glass so the children will know how to sort it. Make as many containers as you need.

Helpful Hint: Keep your trash items large enough to be easily sorted by children. For example, do not include shredded paper.

FUN FACT: AN ENERGY STAR QUALIFIED COMPACT FLUORESCENT LIGHT BULB (CFL) USES 75 PERCENT LESS ENERGY AND CAN LAST UP TO TEN TIMES LONGER THAN AN INCANDESCENT BULB. REPLACING JUST FIVE INCANDESCENT BULBS IN EVERY AMERICAN HOUSEHOLD WITH ENERGY EFFICIENT ONES COULD RESULT IN THE SHUTDOWN OF TWENTY-ONE COAL PLANTS (SOURCE: WWW.ENERGYSTAR.GOV).

Advanced Preparation

You will need to build your garbage pile. If you have a large group, you may prefer to build several piles.

1. Decide how heavy you want your pile to be.

2. Use the following percentages and formula to figure out how much of each type of garbage to add to your large container. These percentages do not equal 100. The remainder is miscellaneous. The math formula is (total weight) × (percentage) = weight of item. *Example:* If we want to figure out how much paper to put into a ten-pound garbage pile, our calculation would look like this: 10 (pounds) × .35 = 3.5 (pounds).

   - paper—35% (.35)
   - metal—8% (.08)
   - glass—7% (.07)
   - plants—18% (.18)
   - food—7% (.07)
   - plastic—10% (.10)
   - shopping bags—1% (.01)
   - wood—7% (.07)

3. After you get all the garbage in the container, mix it up.

4. On each index card, write the name of one item and tape it to a sorting box.

Procedure

Tell the children, "People throw away a lot of stuff. In this activity, we will dig through a garbage pile and find out just how much stuff we throw away." Show the garbage and the sorting boxes to the children. Have them pull items from the garbage pile and decide which box each item belongs in.

Give children a chance to discuss what they found. Ask them which item we throw away the most (paper).

If you have several groups doing this activity, once the last group is finished, leave the garbage sorted. This can be referred to in the lesson on reducing.

B. PAPER PADS FROM SCRAP PAPER (10–15 minutes)

A huge percentage of landfill waste is paper. Even recycling paper takes energy. Here's an option for reusing paper.

Purpose

To reuse scrap paper to make pads of paper or new decorative paper

Materials

- scrap paper with at least one clean side
- paper cutter or scissors
- stapler and staples (CAUTION: stapler for adult use only)
- box
- ink pad (optional)
- small stamps (optional)

Advance Preparation

1. Prior to camp, collect scrap paper that is not wrinkled and has at least one clean side. Advertise at your church for members to donate their scraps.
2. Cut paper to a small, uniform size and place in a box.
3. Determine how many pieces of paper can be stapled together with your stapler.

Procedure

Have children select as many pieces of paper as your stapler can handle. (Optional) Before stacking paper together, children can stamp a small design in a corner of each sheet. Stack the paper neatly and staple together.

(Optional) If children make a lot of pads, consider selling them to church members and donating the money to an environmental charity or using the money to buy a tree to plant.

C. RECYCLED PRESSED PAPER (more than 30 minutes)

Another option is to create artistic pressed paper out of paper scraps. This process is more involved and time-intensive and will appeal to older kids, but it makes a very rewarding product.

Materials

- wooden frame, the size you would like the paper to be, for example, 8 x 10, 5 x 7 or 3½ x 5 (an old picture frame works well for this—remove the back and glass)

- old piece of window screen (to cover the frame)

- lots of used unwaxed/nonglossy paper (newspaper, phone books, envelopes, card stock, and the like)

- basin large enough to hold the frame, at least four inches tall

- blender or hand-sized rocks and old plastic bowls

- one-cup measuring cup

- water

- sponge

- old flannel or felt cloths cut to fit just inside the frame

- dried leaves or flowers (optional)

- two buckets filled halfway with the water

- cardboard or flattened cereal boxes

- plastic butter knife

- food coloring (optional)

- large metal cookie cutters of different shapes that are sharp enough to cut paper (optional)

Advance Preparations

1. Attach the screen to the wooden frame by stapling or nailing it to the frame.

2. Collect plenty of used paper.

3. Collect flowers and leaves and press them for several days (optional).

4. At least two hours prior to making the paper, soak the paper in warm water in a bucket.

Procedure

1. Allow the kids to tear the soaked paper into little tiny pieces and place the pieces into a second bucket filled halfway with water.

2. Scoop out one cup of the small pieces of paper and water and pour into the blender, and add one cup of warm water to the blender. You may also add a few drops of food coloring at this point to color the paper (optional).

3. (Only adults should operate the blender, for safety.) An adult should blend the paper until the mixture becomes a smooth thick pulp with no edges of paper remaining. (An option that does not consume energy is to give each kid a cup of the torn paper and water in a plastic bowl and ask them to crush, grind, and mix it with a rock.)

4. Fill the basin with two inches of warm water.

5. Place the screen in the bottom of the basin with the screen side down.

6. Pour the mixture from the blender over the screen.

7. Gently shake the screen from side to side, leveling out the pulp on the screen (dried flowers or leaves may be added at this time).

8. Raise the screen out of the water to allow water to drain off.

9. Place a felt or flannel cloth on the paper and gently press down to drain more water out of the paper.

10. Take the dry sponge and gently press from beneath the screen to absorb all the water from the paper (you may need to wring the sponge out several times). It is very important that you remove as much water as possible without pushing your hand on the screen (this will cause holes in the paper).

11. With your hand holding the cloth, gently flip the frame over and lay it on the cardboard on a hard surface with the paper still on the cloth.

12. Take the smooth side of the plastic butter knife and gently run it over the entire surface of the screen in order to loosen the paper. (*Note:* if the paper easily pulls away from the screen this step may not be necessary.)

13. Gently remove the frame and leave the paper on the cloth.

14. At this point you might choose to take one of the metal cookie cutters and firmly press it down on the paper to cut the paper into a shape (be careful not to move the paper at all).

15. Allow the paper to dry undisturbed for at least twenty-four hours.

Repeat the steps to make additional sheets of paper.

D. REUSING OLD CLOTHES: SCRAP QUILT MAKING (15–30 minutes)

Purpose

To use old clothes to make sample quilt blocks

Materials

- pictures of scrap quilts or a real quilt (if practical)
- old clothes, of thin cotton
- burlap or other very loose weave fabric (optional)
- large needles (with adult supervision)
- plastic needles (optional)
- thread
- yarn (optional)
- masking tape
- scissors
- permanent marker

Advanced Preparation

Note: If you are working with children who cannot safely use the large needles, use the plastic needles and loose weave cloth or burlap.

1. Cut material into uniform squares.

2. Using the marker, draw a line ½ inch from at least one edge on the wrong side of fabric. *Note:* To quickly draw a line ½ inch from each edge, make a cardboard template that is ½ inch smaller on each side. Place on the wrong side of the fabric and trace around it.

Procedure

Tell the children, "Our ancestors knew how to use old stuff to make something new. When clothes got too old to be worn, people wouldn't throw them away. Instead, they sometimes cut them up and sewed them into quilts."

Show children an actual quilt, if possible, or photos from books. If you have a scrap quilt, you can point out the many different fabrics and imagine with the children what kinds of clothes the fabrics may have come from.

Give each child two squares of fabric. If you are using sharp needles, talk about safety before handing them out. Especially point out that their fingers should not be over the needle as it comes through the fabric.

Demonstrate how to sew the squares together:

1. Place the right sides (sides that are printed) together, so that the lines you drew earlier are on the outside.
2. Use a couple of pieces of tape to hold the fabric together.
3. Thread the needle and knot one end.
4. Sew on the black lines, using a simple running stitch. The stitches do not have to be tiny or uniform.

Pass out needles and pieces of thread. Use yarn if the children are sewing burlap. The children can try to thread the needles, but they will likely need help putting a knot at the end.

Closely supervise children as they sew. If they want to add more to their quilts, allow them to do so, if time permits.

E. SWAP MEET (30 minutes or more, or can be an ongoing activity)

Everyone likes new things, but it takes a lot of energy and resources to make all that new stuff. Rather than buy, children can swap their old things with friends.

Purpose

To organize a swap so children can trade old stuff for new.

Advanced Preparation

1. Decide what you want to swap—perhaps toys, books, board games, DVDs, and video games. Under these big categories, you can subdivide into smaller groups. For

example, toys can be divided into such groups as dolls, building blocks, action figures, and so on.

2. Especially for DVDs and video games, set boundaries for what content and ratings are acceptable.

3. Consider separating older and younger children's items into different swap zones.

Procedure

Decide the procedure for swapping. One way is to operate your swap like a store. Children receive credits when they bring in items. Credits can be given equally, one credit per item, or different items can receive different credit amounts. Items brought in are also priced for a certain number of credits. Children then use the credits they receive to buy "new" items. Another way to determine credits is, rather than charging different credit amounts for different items, give different types of credits to different items, which can then be used to buy like items. For example, a book would receive a book credit, good toward one book.

If you prefer not to use a store model, you can collect all the items brought in for swapping and let the children select items regardless of how much they contributed. You might choose to set a limit on how many items children can select and donate the remainder to a local toy drive.

Decide ahead of time how to settle multiple claims to popular items. One suggestion is to put all the children's names in a hat. Draw a name and let that child select one item. Continue until every child has selected one item. Be sure to keep the names in order if you want to do multiple rounds. Again, decide how many items children can select and donate the rest to charity.

On the day of the swap, set up tables for each category of item. If you are using a store model, clearly mark how many credits an item cost.

Young children, especially, may have a hard time keeping up with credits, so consider making a bracelet with credits.

F. GREETING CARDS (10–15 minutes)

Purpose

To use old greeting cards to make new ones

Materials

- card stock
- used greeting cards
- old calendars
- old magazines
- glue sticks
- scissors
- glitter (optional)
- stickers (optional)
- colored permanent markers

Procedure

Fold the card stock in half. Let the children select pictures to cut from the cards, calendars, and magazines. Have them glue the pictures to the card stock and decorate with glitter, stickers, and markers, if desired.

Optional: As a fundraiser, sell the recycled cards to the congregation and donate the money to an environmental charity.

G. FROM COMICS TO GIFT WRAP (10–15 minutes)

Purpose

To introduce children to the idea of reusing newspaper comics as wrapping paper by practicing with empty boxes

Materials

- colored comics from the newspaper
- scissors
- tape
- small, empty boxes
- scraps of ribbon

Procedure

Give each child an empty box, scissors, and newspaper. Children can cut the paper to size and wrap their boxes, adorning with scraps of ribbon, if desired.

Boxes can be unwrapped and the paper reused for the next child.

H. VISIT A RECYCLING CENTER

Visit your local recycling center to learn how things get recycled. Or go to YouTube and type in "Recycling Center" and select the video titled "From the Curb to the Recycling Center" (http://www.youtube.com/watch?v=62c3Celegq8).

I. PLAN A GROUP GARAGE SALE

Have a group garage sale to recycle items that some no longer want or need but may be appreciated by others. Donate the money to a charity.

SUMMARY AND CLOSING (10–15 minutes)

Debriefing in Small Groups

Use the following questions to guide the discussion:

1. What was your favorite activity that you did today?
2. Why did you like this activity so much?
3. What is something that you learned today?
4. Why do you think it is important to recycle and reuse things more?
5. Why do you think God wants us to take good care of the earth?
6. What kinds of things can we recycle or reuse?
7. What is one item you want to start recycling or reusing more at home and school? Can you think of something that you would enjoy making out of reused items or materials?

CLOSING PRAYER

Dear God: Help us learn to be happy with what we have, to be careful about what we throw away, and to share with others. Amen.

FOUR

Care and Repair of God's Creation

SCRIPTURE TEXTS
Genesis 1:26–31a; Romans 8:21–22

THEME OF THE DAY
Repairing damage done to the earth and replenishing where possible

VERSE OF THE DAY
Be fruitful and multiply and fill the earth (Genesis 1:28)

PURPOSE OF THE LESSON
*To explore ways that all of us can help repair
some of the damage that has been done to the earth.*

FOR THE LEADER—AN OPENING MEDITATION

It doesn't take a rocket scientist to realize that something is severely wrong with our world. In many ways, the earth is sick and in need of healing. And many of the world's problems are human made. So the words of the Apostle Paul take on a whole new meaning: "all of creation groans with pain, like the pain of childbirth" (Romans 8:22, GNT). Our oceans, lakes, and streams are sick with mercury and other toxins. Our air is polluted with carbon emissions and other gases. Our land is being poisoned by pesticides and other chemicals. Our forests are being depleted. Habitats are being destroyed for land development. And through overharvesting and carelessness, some creatures of the sea are being driven into extinction.

That is the bad news. But the good news is there are many practical things that all of us can do to make a positive difference and contribute to the healing of the world. Some of the steps we can take to care for and help heal the earth are simple and easy. Others will be more difficult, requiring significant changes in our lifestyles and habits.

It may not be easy for many of us to make the changes necessary to turn things around in the world. As we all know, it is easier to learn good habits early on than it is to try to break bad habits later on. Thus, the hope of the world may lie in teaching well the young generation, those in elementary and middle school.

So let's get started exploring ways that all of us can help care for creation by repairing and replenishing!

GATHERING TIME

Purpose

To introduce the concept of repairing by giving children broken things to fix

Gathering Music

"All Things Bright and Beautiful" (*New Century Hymnal*, #31) or another familiar hymn

Materials

- items that need simple, quick repairs, such as toys that need to be cleaned, bird houses that need a fresh coat of paint, and books with torn pages
- items for making repairs, including small paint brushes, nontoxic paint, newspapers, and containers for water (such as butter tubs), cleaning rags, liquid soap, and transparent tape
- CD player
- CD with Gathering Music
- bag of candy
- small serving bowl
- large sheet of paper
- marker
- masking tape

Advance Preparations

1. Spread newspapers over your work area.

2. Set out the items that need repairs with the materials for repairing them.

3. Solicit volunteers to assist children in their repairs.

4. Fill a bowl with candy, but do not set on the work area; keep extra candy handy.

5. Write the verse of the day on a large sheet of paper and hang it.

GETTING STARTED (10–15 minutes)

Play the music in the background. As the children arrive, direct them to the work area. Let each child select something to repair, and assign a volunteer to help.

After all the children have arrived and have had a few minutes to work on their projects, ask them to leave the projects at the work area and assemble in a circle for Sharing Time.

SHARING TIME

(Children may be divided into small groups.)

Materials

- book: *A River Ran Wild: An Environmental History* by Lynne Cherry
- story (printed below): "A Special Tree" by Randy Hammer
- Bibles
- copy of discussion questions

A. DISCOVERING CONTEMPORARY EXPERIENCES OF REPAIRING AND REPLENISHING

Sharing My Life (5–10 minutes)

Purpose

To introduce children to the concept of replenishing and repairing

Opening Small Group Questions

Think of an important item from your life that was broken. Be prepared to share your experience as you discuss the following questions with your small group:

1. Ask the children to talk about what they were doing at the work table. What were they fixing? How was it broken?

2. How did you feel about the broken object?

3. Were you able to repair or restore it?

4. If you were able to repair it, was it just like it was originally or was it changed?

5. How did you feel about being able to fix your object?

Tell the group that today we are going to be talking about how the earth is "broken" and ways we can help repair it. Remind them that to repair something means to fix it.

Walk around with the bowl of candy and let each child take one.

When each child has taken candy, point out that when you started, the bowl was full; now it is empty, or nearly so. Take extra candy and refill the bowl.

Ask the children what you did. Tell them that another word for refilling is replenishing. Replenish means to fill something up again or restore it. Today's lesson will also talk about how we can replenish the earth's resources, plants, and animals.

Sharing Others' Experiences of Repairing and Replenishing (15–30 minutes)

Purpose

To explore ways people have repaired the earth

Procedure

Choose one of the following stories. If your group is planning an outing to clean a stream or plant a tree (Activities G and H), choose the story that corresponds to that activity as an introduction to your service project.

Story One (to introduce Activity G)

"A Special Tree" by Randy Hammer (from *The Talking Stick: 40 Children's Sermons with Activities*, Cleveland: Pilgrim Press, 2007)

"Amanda, how about you help me with a little job this morning," Amanda's dad said just as they were finishing their Saturday morning breakfast.

"Do I have to?" Amanda said wearily. "Saturday is the only day I have to watch cartoons. Besides, I don't like to work."

"It won't take long," her dad assured. "And we'll have fun together, I promise."

Amanda rolled her eyes. "Oh, all right, if it won't take long."

A few minutes later Amanda and her dad were standing on the sidewalk near the street with two shovels, one for each of them. "Right here will be a good spot for our new tree," Amanda's dad said as he drew a circle on the ground with the point of his shovel. "Let's start digging." Amanda's dad showed her how to point the shovel in the dirt and place her foot on the shovel to exert pressure and push down. After a couple of digs, Amanda was finding shoveling to be quite fun and satisfying.

Fifteen minutes later, they stood before a round hole in the ground about as big as a beach ball. "Well, that should be big enough," Amanda's dad said. "Let's get the tree." He opened the back of the van, eased out a six-foot-tall tree and carried it to the hole. Carefully they positioned the tree in the hole so it was standing just right and filled in the hole with the loose dirt they had dug. Then they covered the soil with mulch and with the water hose gave it a good drink.

"Now, doesn't that look nice?" Amanda's dad quizzed. Amanda had to agree that it did. "But there's one more thing we have to do."

"Oh no, more work?" Amanda complained.

"Well, not really," her dad said as he pulled something from his back pocket. It was a small metal sign.

"What's that?" Amanda asked.

"Well, I'm glad you asked that," her dad replied. "This is an honorary plaque that shows that this tree was planted to honor someone who is very special. Every person who walks by this tree can read this sign and think good thoughts about the person whose name is on it."

Now Amanda was really curious. "Who does it honor?" she asked excitedly. "Whose name is on the plaque?"

"Well, why don't you read it for yourself?" her dad invited.

Amanda took the metal sign in her hand and read out loud: "This tree has been planted in honor of Amanda Smith."

As Amanda's dad took the plaque and carefully placed it in the ground near the tree, she was proud—proud of her dad's love, proud she had learned to shovel, and proud that he had wanted to plant a tree in her honor.

Questions for Discussion

1. What happened in this story?

2. Why do you think Amanda's dad wanted to plant the tree?

3. Why do we need trees?

4. Is planting a tree something you think you could do?

Story Two (to introduce Activity H)

A River Ran Wild: An Environmental History by Lynne Cherry

Tell the group, "Sometimes when we look at the damage we've done to the earth, we think that's such a big problem, there's no way we can fix it. But all it takes is one person with a dream of how clean the earth can be. When that person shares the dream, other people want to help, too. If we keep trying, we might find that we can fix those big problems. The book we're going to read is about a river that got so dirty that nothing could live in it anymore and people wouldn't go near it. But someone had a dream that it could be cleaned. Let's read what happened."

Read the book to the children, taking time to talk about the pictures. If your time is short or you have a young audience, you may want to abbreviate the story. However, keep the key elements: the change from the river's being clean to dirty to clean again, and the work of people to clean up the pollution.

Questions for Discussion

1. How did the river look at the beginning of the story? What animals used the river? How did people use the river?

2. How did the river change after the factories moved in? How was the river used? What happened to the animals?

3. How did the river look at the end of the story? How did the river get cleaned? What lives there now? How do people use the river now?

B. DISCOVERING A BIBLICAL VIEW OF REPAIRING AND REPLENISHING (15–30 minutes)

Tell your group, "Humans have not always done a good job of taking care of the earth. Let's read these verses and talk about how we might fix some of the problems."

Read Genesis 1:26–31a as a group.

Questions for Discussion

1. What do you think it means that humans were created in God's image or likeness?

2. How do you think God feels about all of creation—including people, animals, and plants (verse 31)?

3. What kinds of things did God create on the earth to give to humans to take care of?

4. God set a plan in place for providing plants and trees to feed humans and the animals (verses 29–30). What do you think would happen if green plants and fruit trees started to get sick and disappear? How would it affect humans and animals if there were fewer plants and trees? (Answers include a shrinking food supply, more CO^2 in the air.)

Next read Romans 8:21–22 as a group.

Questions for Discussion

1. Do you think the earth is in as good a shape as it used to be?

2. In what ways do you think the earth is broken and hurting? Try to think of some specific ways.

3. How do you think God feels about the bad shape the earth is in and how it will affect us as we live in the pollution?

4. Can you think of some ways we can help repair the earth and replenish its natural resources?

C. ENCOURAGING CHILDREN'S CREATIVITY (15–30 minutes)

Purpose

To learn about the importance of trees

Materials

- large sheet of brown paper or used brown paper bags
- green construction paper
- dark markers
- large sheet of white paper
- scissors

- tape
- *The Gift of the Tree* by Alvin Tresselt or *A Grand Old Tree* by Mary Newell DePalma (*A Grand Old Tree* is more accessible for younger audiences)

Advance Preparation

1. Cut a tree trunk, with branches, from the brown paper or paper bags and tape it to the wall.

2. Decide how many leaves you want for the tree, then draw enough large, simple leaves on the construction paper. If your paper is 9 x 12 inches, draw two leaves per sheet. Children will cut the leaves out later.

Procedure

Read the book to the children. Say, "Today we are going to write a giant thank-you to trees for all the gifts they give to the earth. In a moment, you will get a piece of paper with a leaf drawn on it. I want you to write on your leaf one thing that trees give us. Make sure that all your words are inside the leaf because then you are going to cut them out and tape them to our tree trunk."

Next, brainstorm with the children ideas of gifts trees give the earth. You can refer to the following list for help. Write the ideas on the large, white paper.

Distribute the construction paper, markers, and scissors to the children. Encourage children to create multiple leaves.

When the children are finished, let them cut the leaves out and attach them to the tree, using the tape.

The following is an incomplete list of the benefits of trees, or the gifts they give. Feel free to add any gifts you might think of.

- shade
- beauty, especially in autumn
- nest holder
- safe place for animals
- replenishers of soil
- food for mushrooms and other fungi

- home to carpenter ants, termites, deer mice, chipmunks, raccoons, and birds
- place for moss to grow
- food for grubs, beetles, centipedes, snails, slugs, earthworms
- seeds for new trees
- paper
- wood for furniture, homes, and toys
- maple syrup
- cleaners of the air
- givers of oxygen
- erosion prevention
- food for birds and mammals (including apples, oranges, bananas, limes, lemons, grapefruit, mangoes, papayas, olives, cherries, plums, apricots, peaches, walnuts, pecans, almonds)

ACTIVITY TIME

A. WHAT'S SO IMPORTANT ABOUT SEEDS? (15–30 minutes)

Purpose

To introduce the marvel of seeds to children and the idea that nature replenishes itself

Materials

for Part One: Exploring the Seeds

- packages of seeds
- magnifying glasses
- flowers/plants that have gone to seed (sunflowers are great, but other flowers and weeds work well)
- dandelion gone to seed or another seed (maple, milkweed) that travels by air

for Part Two: Exploring the Fruit

- variety of fruits and vegetables with seeds
- cutting board
- knife, wrapped in a towel (CAUTION: Do not allow children to handle the knife. Explain that knives can hurt us and should only be used by an adult.)
- paper plate to hold cut fruit
- napkins for each student
- hand cleaner

Note: You can incorporate this activity into snack time. Make sure all the food is clean and children have washed their hands. Provide a healthy snack dip, if you like.

Part One: Exploring the Seeds

Say, "We used the word 'replenish' today. Who can tell me what that means?" (To make full or complete again) "Nature is very good at replenishing itself. Now we are going to look at how plants replenish themselves."

Ask, "Has anyone ever planted flower or vegetable seeds?" Show children the seed package and say, "Maybe you planted seeds from a package like this." Ask, "Have you ever wondered where seeds come from before they go in the packages?"

Hand out magnifying glasses and show children flowers that have gone to seed. Say, "Plants make the seeds." Allow children time to look at seeds.

Point out to children, "Look how many seeds there are on this one flower. Why do you think the flower makes that many seeds?" (Because many seeds won't have a chance to grow. You can explore reasons why this is so. For example, a seed might land on soil that's not good, or it might be eaten.)

Show the children the dandelion with seeds, "Look at the fluff on these seeds. What do you think that is for?" (To help the seed move away from the parent plant on the wind and to land in a spot that isn't so crowded.)

Part Two: Exploring the Fruit

Say, "Sometimes seeds are easy to find, but sometimes they are hidden inside fruits and vegetables." Show children the variety of fruits and vegetables and say, "Let's cut open some of these fruits and look at the seeds. Before we do, can you guess which fruit will have the largest seed and which will have the smallest?"

Let the children vote on which fruit has the largest seed and the smallest. They can line the foods up in order from largest seed to smallest.

For each fruit and vegetable, cut it in half and let the children see how it looks inside. Point out the seeds. Then cut the fruit in bite-size pieces and let the children sample them.

B. PLANTING SEEDS (10–15 minutes)

Purpose

To follow up on the seed exploration and to introduce the idea that humans need to replenish plants when they harvest too many.

Materials

- packages of seeds
- potting soil (choose a soil that is made for starting seeds)
- cardboard egg cartons or other recycled container
- scoop or small yogurt cup
- water

- small pitcher
- newspaper

Advance Preparation

Cut the egg cartons into smaller sections.

Procedure

Tell the children that humans use plants for a lot of things, such as making paper and houses and for food. We have learned that if we use a lot of plants, we need to help replenish them by planting seeds.

Let the children help cover their work area with newspaper (or work outside). Give each child a section of egg carton and enough seeds to put two in each cup. Let the children fill each cup with soil, plant the seeds according to package instructions, and water until the soil is moist.

If the children take the seeds home, remind them that the soil needs to stay moist so the seeds will sprout.

C. LITTER RACE (10–15 minutes)

Purpose

To reinforce the idea that litter belongs in the garbage or recycling bin.

Materials

- newspapers
- several small garbage cans or recycling bins
- timer
- whistle
- plastic gallon milk jugs

Advanced Preparation

1. Select a playing area and litter it with wadded up newspapers.
2. Place the garbage cans/recycling bins on the outside of the playing area.

3. Cut away part of the milk jugs to make scoops. Make sure you leave the handles on your scoops and that the cut edges are not sharp.

Procedure

The object of the game is to put as much litter in your can as possible. Each round of play can have as many children as you have garbage cans.

When the whistle blows, each child runs on the field and picks up one piece of litter at a time and brings it in the garbage can. When the whistle blows again, or when all the litter is picked up, whoever has the most litter in the can wins.

Note: To make this more challenging, give children milk carton scoops to scoop up the litter without touching it with their hands.

D. OIL SPILL CLEAN-UP (10–15 minutes, or longer, if desired)

Purpose

Sometimes, repairing damage to the environment is a huge undertaking. This activity gives children an idea of what is involved in cleaning up an oil spill.

Materials

- vegetable oil
- bowls
- water
- cotton balls
- sponges
- baby powder
- paper towels
- spoons
- cocoa (optional)

Note: You can add a little cocoa to the vegetable oil to make a darker oil.

Procedure

Tell children that we use oil for lots of things. We make gasoline from it to run our cars and other machines. We also use it to make plastic, ink, crayons, dishwashing liquid,

FUN FACT: ONE LARGE TREE CAN ABSORB ONE TON OF CO_2 OVER ITS LIFETIME.

CDs and DVDs, tires, and even bubblegum! Usually that oil has to be carried a long way, either by ship or truck. Sometimes an accident happens and the oil leaks out. When it does, it pollutes the ground or the water, and it has to be cleaned up.

Put water in the bowls and add some vegetable oil. Next, the children need to figure out how to get the oil off the water. They can choose any combination of the supplies and experiment with them.

Afterward, talk with children about what they've done and how successful they were.

E. CLEANING ANIMALS CAUGHT IN OIL SPILLS (10–15 minutes)

Purpose

To help children understand that oil spills affect other creatures and that humans can help repair the damage.

Materials

- one small container
- one large container, about the size of a dish tub
- vegetable oil
- cocoa
- old socks (one per child)
- old rags or stuffing
- toothbrushes
- washcloths
- sponges
- hand dishwashing liquid
- permanent marker

Advanced Preparation

For each child, make a sock animal by stuffing old socks with rags or stuffing. Knot the end. Make fake petroleum by mixing vegetable oil and cocoa, using three parts oil and two parts cocoa.

Procedure

First add water to the small container, then slowly add the oil/cocoa mixture. This represents the oil spill.

Next, add water and dishwashing liquid to the larger container. This is the bath water.

Give each child a stuffed sock. Let the child draw an animal on it with permanent markers. Explain that when pollution gets in the water that it can harm animals. Let children dip their animals in the oily water. Tell the children that people help to repair the damage by cleaning these animals. Give children cleaning tools and let them bathe their animals.

Discuss with children: Was it easy to get the oil off? How might the oil harm the animals? (The oil can poison them if they try to lick it off. The oil ruins their water repellence.)

F. INVITE AN ENVIRONMENTALIST

Invite a local environmentalist to talk about ways the local environment is being cleaned up.

G. PLANT A TREE

In advance, speak to a homeowner in the neighborhood near the church, explaining the lesson series. Ask if your church can plant some trees in their yard as a service project. At the end of the lesson, walk over to the house and plant the trees. Make sure to research ahead of time the best type of tree to plant, the best place in the yard to plant them, and how to care for the trees. The website www.tlcfortrees.info/ gives helpful advice about selecting, planting, and caring for trees.

H. CLEAN UP!

Schedule a group trip to a local creek or park to pick up trash. Make sure everyone wears thick gloves. Bring separate trash bags for items that can be recycled and for trash.

SUMMARY AND CLOSING (10–15 minutes)

Debriefing in Small Groups

Use the following questions to guide the discussion:

1. What was your favorite activity today?

2. Why do you think we did the activities?

3. What are some parts of the earth that are broken and sick?

4. What are some ways we talked about today that we can help repair and replenish the earth's natural resources?

5. What is one thing you learned today that you can do to help the earth?

CLOSING PRAYER

Creator God: We want to help keep the earth beautiful and clean. We want the earth to be healthy and whole. Let us be shown ways that we can make changes in our lives and help heal the earth. Amen.

FIVE

Consumption of God's Creation

SCRIPTURE TEXTS
Exodus 16:4–8, 13–21 (GNT suggested)

THEME OF THE DAY
Learning to reduce what we consume

VERSE OF THE DAY
Use only what you need. (based on Exodus 16:16)

PURPOSE OF THE LESSON
*To learn ways that we can reduce what we consume
for the overall good of our world.*

FOR THE LEADER—AN OPENING MEDITATION

We invite you to read the ancient story of manna in the wilderness in a whole new light. Instead of focusing on the miracle of God's providing food for the Hebrew people, focus on the people's response. The injunction is repeated throughout that the people are to gather just enough for the day, with the only exception being on the sixth day when extra could be gathered for the Sabbath. To put it another way, each family was to gather just what was needed, no more, no less; they were not to hoard. When the people got greedy and gathered more than they needed, the outcome was wormy, rotten food, incurring the anger of Moses.

The lesson for our society today is that we also can reduce our consumption and learn to take and use only what we really need from the earth. We can learn to be more careful to not hoard and pile up and toss away that which is not really necessary. We may not need to buy so many prepackaged foods when we have the option of enjoying fresh fruits and vegetables, especially those locally grown. We do not need to "hoard" heating fuel by having our thermostats turned so high when a sweater would keep us just as warm. We do not need to use more gas than necessary for our automobiles, when we could plan ahead and combine trips or carpool and even buy a more efficient car in the future. By now, you probably are getting the picture. Use only as needed. Do not hoard. Do not be greedy. Reduce what you consume and throw away.

These are ideas that we will explore in this lesson. So let's get started learning new ways to reduce our consumption for the betterment of our earth!

GATHERING TIME

Purpose

To provide an experience of "too much," in order to talk about reducing

Gathering Music

"De Colores, 'Sing of Colors'" (*New Century Hymnal,* #402) or another familiar hymn

Materials

- several very small suitcases or boxes
- items to pack for each suitcase, including necessities and luxuries (*Note:* You will need more items than can fit in the suitcases.)
- CD player
- CD with Gathering Music

Advance Preparations

1. Set the suitcases with items to pack on the floor.

2. Write the verse of the day on a large sheet of paper and hang.

3. Provide seating, as for Lesson One.

GETTING STARTED (5–10 minutes)

Play the music softly in the background, as children arrive. As each child arrives, direct him or her to a suitcase. Tell children to pack as much as they can. They will have to choose what to pack and what to leave out. *Note:* Do not try to influence their choices.

When all the children have arrived and suitcases are packed, move into Sharing Time.

SHARING TIME

Materials

- large pot
- book: *One Potato, Two Potato* by Cynthia DeFelice
- copy paper for each child or one large sheet of paper
- crayons or markers
- tape

A. DISCOVERING CONTEMPORARY IDEAS ABOUT REDUCING WHAT WE USE

Sharing My Life (5–10 minutes)

Purpose

Using the suitcase activity to help children distinguish between necessities and luxuries

Opening Small Group Questions

1. Ask the children how their packing went. Were they able to get everything in the suitcase? What things did they choose to pack and what did they leave out?

2. Next, say, "Imagine that you are at home one day and your parents come in your room and tell you that there is an emergency and your family must leave in ten minutes and they do not know when you will be able to return. In that ten minutes you are to pack only one suitcase and nothing more. What would you pack?"

3. Ask children to look at what they packed. Would they make different choices now? Help them think about what they might need during an emergency.

4. Tell the children that things we need to stay alive are called necessities. What are some necessities in your pile of stuff? Things we like to have, but don't need, are called luxuries. What are some luxuries in your pile?

5. Say, "When we talk about reducing what we use to help the earth, what things could we reduce first?"

Sharing Others' Experiences of Reducing Our Consumption (15–30 minutes)

Purpose

To begin thinking about what it means to be satisfied when you have enough

Procedure

Either hand out paper and crayons or attach a large sheet of paper to the wall. Place a large pot in the middle of the group. Tell the children to imagine that this is a magic pot and anything you put in it will be doubled. The pot will keep working for as long as you want.

Ask children to think of what they would like to put in the pot. They can either draw pictures to share or you can write their ideas on a large sheet of paper.

Say, "Let's read a story about two people who found such a pot and what they did with it." Read *One Potato, Two Potato* by Cynthia DeFelice.

Discuss the book with the children. Two important concepts for them to discover are that the couple was not selfish with the pot, but put it back for others to use, and that friendship was more important than things.

B. DISCOVERING A BIBLICAL VIEW ABOUT REDUCING OUR CONSUMPTION (15–30 minutes)

Say to the children, "We have been talking about the difference between things you need and things you want. We've also read a story about two people who were satisfied when they had just enough. Let's read some Bible verses that also talk about taking just what you need."

Read Exodus 16:4–8, 13–21 (GNT) as a group.

Questions for Discussion

1. What happens in the passage? What does God instruct the Israelites to do?

2. What happened when the Israelites tried to keep too much food until morning?

3. Have you ever seen fruit or other food go bad? What happens? Is it a pleasant sight? Why do you think food goes bad?

4. Why do you think God wanted the people to collect only as much as they needed for one day? (To learn to trust and depend on God for all they needed on a daily basis, so nothing would be wasted)

5. What do you think happens when people today try to collect more things than they need (more food, clothing, shelter, possessions, etc. than they need or can possibly use)? (A lot is wasted; those people use more natural resources than they should; other people go without)

6. Can you think of a way you can start to take and use just as much as you need? (Examples: only take as much food as you can eat; only buy clothes when you really need them)

C. ENCOURAGING CHILDREN'S CREATIVITY (15–30 minutes)

Purpose

To start children thinking about small steps they can take to reduce their energy consumption.

Materials

- copy paper
- construction paper (9 x 12)
- markers or crayons
- large sheet of paper
- marker
- glue sticks
- masking tape

Note: This activity can be prepared as a bulletin board display.

Procedure

Introduce the activity by telling the group that many things we do every day take energy. It takes energy to drive a car, to heat water, to wash our clothes, to cook our food, and to watch TV. We can make small changes that help reduce how much energy we use. For example, we can hang clothes to dry instead of putting them in the dryer. Ask if they can think of other ways to reduce our energy use.

Tape the large sheet of paper to the wall and write down ideas that the children have. Some suggestions include the following:

- Rewear clothes that aren't dirty.
- Use a reusable water bottle.
- Take a shorter shower.
- Help hang up wet clothes to dry.
- Turn off lights when I leave a room.
- Turn off electronics when I'm finished.
- Play a game that doesn't need electricity.
- Read a book.
- Choose fresh fruit over canned fruit.

Next, put the paper and crayons/markers in the center of the work area and let the children help themselves. Instruct them to choose an idea from the list or make one up for themselves. The idea should be a way to reduce how much energy they use.

They should write the phrase, "Tomorrow, I Can (fill in the blank)," at the top of their paper, then draw a picture to correspond to it.

If you are making a display, they can glue their pictures to construction paper, then add to the bulletin board or tape to a wall with masking tape.

Note: You may want to move the snack activity here (Activity D below).

ACTIVITY TIME

A. AN HONEST COMMERCIAL (FOR OLDER ELEMENTARY) (15–30 minutes)

Purpose

To help children understand that the purpose of advertisements is to sell products, and to help them learn to judge for themselves whether they really need something.

Materials

- various objects about which to make an honest commercial, such as healthy food, junk food, a jump rope, an action figure, building blocks. (Children could also make a commercial about a product that was bought because the advertisement made it seem much better than it really was.)

- paper

- pencils

- poster board

- markers

- video camera (optional)

- TV or computer to view video (optional)

- samples of advertisements, especially toy ads that make products look better than they are

Procedure

Begin by discussing with the children what an advertisement is. Next, relate to the children an experience of your own when you bought something based on an ad, but which turned out not to be what you expected. Or you can use the following example:

"When I was young, there was a commercial on TV for a cereal. The little boy eating the cereal seemed to be enjoying it so much that I decided I wanted some, too. I asked my mother to buy me some. She told me that she knew it wasn't a very tasty cereal, but I insisted that it must be delicious because the boy on TV loved it. So my mother bought the cereal and fixed it and I took one bite. It was yucky! That's when I learned that TV commercials and other advertisements are not always honest!"

FUN FACT: ADJUSTING YOUR THERMOSTAT BY TWO DEGREES SAVES OVER 1200 LITERS OF CO_2 EMISSIONS EACH DAY.

Divide the children into small groups and give each group a product. Let the groups explore their objects and write down true statements about them. The statements should look at the positive and negative aspects. For example, a piece of junk food may be delicious, but it can also contribute to cavities and it isn't nutritious.

After the groups have several aspects listed, give them poster board and markers and tell them to make an honest ad about that product. Let the groups share their ads. (Optional) Children can make a commercial rather than a printed ad. If you have the equipment, you can make a video of it.

Discuss with the children what they learned about advertisements. Discuss how not being swayed by fancy ads helps us to make smarter choices and reduce what we buy. When we reduce what we buy, we help the earth because it takes resources to make everything.

Extension: You can have children make two advertisements about their product, one that presents the product as better than it really is, as well as the honest ad.

B. PAPER CUTTING (ESPECIALLY FOR YOUNGER ELEMENTARY) (15–30 minutes)

Purpose

Children have learned that a lot of paper is thrown away (Lesson 3, Garbage Archeology). This activity will help them learn one way to use paper wisely, while making a fun craft.

Materials

- construction paper
- pencils
- scissors
- dowel rods
- knife (optional)
- wood glue (optional)

- string (optional)
- thin string or heavy thread
- scotch tape
- cardboard templates of simple animal shape.
- paper templates of ovals (see note)

Note: The oval should be approximately one-fourth the size of the construction paper. Each child will need four ovals, so have enough for all the children in a small group to work at the same time. If time is short, skip Part One, but monitor children closely, to guide them in using paper efficiently.

Procedure

This is a two-part activity. In Part One, children will learn how to fit ovals on the paper to get maximum use of the paper. In Part Two, they will apply this skill to make a mobile with the least amount of paper waste.

Part One

Note: To save paper, children do not need to cut the ovals from the construction paper.

Procedure

Give each child a sheet of construction paper and one oval. Ask them to put the oval on the paper like they would if they were going to cut it out. Do not guide them as to where to put the oval; let the activity teach them.

Now give each child a second oval and tell them to add it to the paper. Ovals should not overlap. Children may have to move the first oval to fit both.

Give each child a third oval and have them do the same.

Finally, give them the fourth oval.

Let children talk with you about how placing ovals near the edges and corners of the paper lets them get the most ovals on the paper.

Part Two

With adult guidance, children will apply the lesson they learned in Part One and cut shapes to make a mobile. You can make a simple mobile with just one dowel rod or a more complex mobile with two dowel rods crossed and tied.

Advance Preparation

If you are making a more complex mobile with two rods, first use a knife to make notches at the center point of each dowel rod. Working with one pair at a time, put a small bit of wood glue in the notches and cross the rods and use the string to bind them together. (CAUTION: Knife for adult use only; always cut away from your body.)

Procedure

Give each child a pair of scissors and a pencil. The construction paper and templates should be accessible to all.

Tell the children, "We are going to practice our paper saving skills and make a mobile at the same time." (If children do not know what a mobile is, explain this.)

Instruct them to choose any of the templates that they like, trace around them, and cut them out. As they are working, make sure they are placing the templates close to edges and corners to save paper. Encourage them to use scrap pieces of paper that are big enough rather than always choosing a new piece.

Once their shapes have been cut out, let the children cut enough pieces of string or heavy thread to hang the shapes. Tape the string to the shapes and rods for the finished mobiles.

C. PUT ON A SWEATER (WHY WEARING A SWEATER CAN SAVE ENERGY) (10–15 minutes)

Purpose

Keeping our homes cooler in the winter will save energy. This exercise will show children how a sweater can insulate their bodies and keep them warm, even when the temperatures are cooler. *Note:* Because of the hot water involved, this exercise should be done as a demonstration in a small group.

Materials

- two glass jars of the same size with tight fitting lids
- very hot water (adult only)
- funnel
- oven mitt
- two thermometers

- wool sock (big enough to cover one jar)
- scraps of paper
- marker

Say to the children: "Today we have been talking about reducing the amount of energy we use. One easy thing we can do to save energy is to keep our homes cooler in the winter. Sometimes kids don't want to do this because they get cold. But have your parents ever told you to put on a sweater when you're cold? They say that for a good reason.

"Remember when we talked about the polar bear?" (Lesson One) "What does the polar bear have that helps it keep warm?" (blubber and two types of fur). "So the polar bear is comfortable outside, even when the temperature drops to 34 degrees below zero. But people don't have blubber and fur, so what happens to us when it's cold?

"So since we don't have built-in blubber and fur, we have to put extra layers of clothes on our bodies to stay warm. Let's find out how important those layers are.

Procedure

Show the children the jars and sock. Point out that the sock is like a sweater for the jar. Leave one jar as it is. Cover the second jar with the sock.

Pour very hot water into both jars. (CAUTION: For safety, one adult should hold the funnel using an oven mitt while a second adult pours the water, also using an oven mitt. Do not allow the children to assist in this.) Set a thermometer in each jar. Read the temperature in each jar and let a child write it on a scrap of paper.

Remove the thermometers and fasten the lids securely on the jars.

After thirty minutes, check the temperature in each jar again. Write down the new temperature on the scraps of paper. Was there a change? Which changed more?

Talk with the children about what this exercise shows us about wearing a sweater when it's cold.

D. COMPARING SINGLE-SERVE AND MULTISERVE PACKAGING OF THE SAME ITEM (15–30 minutes)

Purpose

To help children learn to choose products with less packaging and to stress environmentally sound choices over convenience.

Note 1: Incorporate this activity into snack time.

Note 2: Making the best choice is not always obvious. When you buy multiserve items for a large group, you need to factor in napkins or plates for the snack and cups for the drink. Ideally, choose washable, reusable ware, but if that's not practical, choose items made from recycled materials, if it is not cost prohibitive. At the very least, choose recyclable cups and thin napkins. Remember that paper plates and napkins are not recyclable, and disposable foam products often are not, as well.

Materials

- single-serve snacks and drinks for half the group
- multiserve snacks and drinks for half the group
- cups and napkins or plates for the multiserve half (see note 2)
- plastic sandwich baggie
- reusable container with lid
- paper bag
- lunch box
- juice box
- reusable drink bottle
- paper napkin
- cloth napkin

Procedure

Explain to the children that shopping gives us many opportunities to make choices that are better for the earth. Once you get past the fruits and vegetables in a grocery store, everything you buy comes in a package. And that package is just going to be thrown away. So when we pick our foods, we can think about how much packaging we're buying and then try to buy less of that packaging. Say, "Our snack today will help us look at one choice we can make."

Divide kids into two groups. Give the first group single-serve snacks and drinks. Give the second group napkins or plates and cups. Pass out snacks and pour drinks. They should get the same amount of food as the first group.

After the children have eaten, instruct them to sort their trash into recyclable and nonrecyclable piles. Compare the sizes of the piles for each group. Give the children an opportunity to respond.

Then lay out the baggie, reusable container, paper bag, lunchbox, juice box, drink bottle, paper napkin and cloth napkin. Tell the children that sometimes we buy single-serve items because it's easier. Now we know that easier isn't always better. But if you want to pack a lunch, you can't put a huge bag of snacks in there, can you? What could do? (Transfer the amount you need to a smaller container.)

Show the kids the various disposable and the reusable lunchbox items. Say, "We know that if we buy a big box of something, we'll have to put small amounts of it in something else so we can take it in our lunch boxes. Which should we choose?" Show the various items and let the children decide which is better for the earth. Help them understand which items can be washed and used again and which will be thrown away.

E. PUT THE SUN TO WORK! (10–15 minutes)

Purpose

Developing alternative sources of energy is a big step we can take to help the environment. This activity introduces children to the idea that the sun provides us with energy.

Materials

- ice cubes (you will need two of the same size for each child)
- a sunny day
- samples of photovoltaic cells, such as solar powered calculators (optional)

Procedure

Tell the group that sunlight is energy. One thing that energy can do is heat things. (Make sure they understand what it means to heat something.) Show children an ice cube and ask: "What happens when an ice cube gets warm? Let's see if the sunlight makes an ice cube melt faster."

Give each child two ice cubes and instruct the children to place one in the bright sun and the other in a dark place. Have them keep track of how quickly each cube melts.

Dialogue with children about the experiment. *Note:* Children will notice that both ice cubes melt. Remind them that the sun's energy warms our whole planet.

(Optional) Show children the photovoltaic cells. Tell them that the sun's energy can be used just as it is, such as heating our homes when it shines through the windows, but we can also use the cells to turn that sunlight directly into electricity.

SUMMARY AND CLOSING (10–15 minutes)

Debriefing in Small Groups

Use the following questions to guide the discussion:

1. What new fact did you learn today?

2. Did you think of something that you could use less of? If so, what?

3. Can you think of a time when you used far too much of something and then wished you had not?

4. Can you remember a time when you took or used less, and felt really good about it?

5. What is one small way that you might change so as to use less and share more?

CLOSING PRAYER

O Creator: We have learned that there are things we can do to improve our world. So help us to live simpler lives and to use less and to share more with others who have less. Amen.

SIX

Living in God's Creation

SCRIPTURE TEXTS
Matthew 6:25–34; Matthew 7:12

THEME OF THE DAY
Learning to live more simply and with less

VERSE OF THE DAY
"Do not worry about your life." (Matthew 6:25)

PURPOSE OF THE LESSON
Because the earth's resources are limited,
children will learn ways to live simpler lives and
to share resources with those who have less.

FOR THE LEADER—AN OPENING MEDITATION

It pays to watch what you eat. This we are learning more and more. There are some foods that we may enjoy (red meats high in fat content, doughnuts, fast food meals, and so on) but that are just not as healthy for us to eat. Although in previous generations such foods may have been consumed without much thought, and in some cases people thought they were eating healthily, we now know there is a better way. By eating more fruits and vegetables and less red meat, sugar, and processed foods, we may feel better, have fewer illnesses, and live longer.

Changing the way we eat can also impact the world at large. By eating more of such things as beans and rice and locally grown fruits and vegetables, we help improve our world. Meat production generates more greenhouse gas emissions than transportation, and 70 percent of the former forests in the Amazon are used for grazing. It takes many times more resources—grain that could be used to feed humans, water, land space—to produce beef than it does rice and beans. And consuming items that are trucked great distances may add to the pollution problem.

Most of us enjoy going out occasionally for an expensive meal with family and friends. But what if we decided to eat out a little less, and in moderation, and instead eat a simple meal at home? By so doing, we can have a small, but positive, impact on our earth and its limited resources.

One of the teachings of Jesus is to worry less about acquiring the things of life and to learn to live simpler lives. Today's lesson will introduce children to the unequal distribution of resources among nations and focus on how we can conserve one resource—water. As the great humanitarian Mahatma Gandhi put it, "There is enough for the world's need but not enough for the world's greed." So let's get started in exploring ways that all of us can be more mindful of the resources of God's wonderful creation as we seek to live simpler lives.

GATHERING TIME

Purpose

To provide children with an experience of how the world's resources are disproportionately distributed so they can begin thinking about how much we have in our country compared to other countries

Gathering Music

"I've Got Peace Like a River" (*New Century Hymnal,* #478) or another familiar hymn

Materials

- tables, each set up for approximately eight children
- country name cards for each table
- masking tape, for hanging banners

- different sizes of paper (large art or butcher paper to 8½ x 11 paper)
- many different art supplies (see instructions that follow)
- candy for all the children
- CD player
- CD with Gathering Music

Advance Preparations

1. Set up tables and label them as different countries. (The idea is to differentiate between some wealthy countries that use most of the world's resources and poor countries that do not have many resources. Wealthy countries are A, B, C, D, and E, and poor countries are F, G, H, I, and J.)

2. Write the verse of the day on a large sheet of paper and hang it.

3. Provide seating, as for Lesson One.

GETTING STARTED (15–30 minutes)

Play the music softly in the background, as children arrive. As they arrive, assign each child to a "country" and ask the children to sit at that table. (Do not assign tables based on small groups. Assign the tables randomly as the children arrive or by numbering the children off). Each table should have no more than eight children.

When everyone has arrived, give the children the following instructions: "We are going to make banners about reducing the amount of natural resources we use. Natural resources are things that come from nature that we can use. Water is a natural resource. Can you think of others?" (Allow children time to respond.) "We will be passing out paper and supplies you can use to decorate your country's banner."

Instruct the children that they may look at what other countries are making, but they may not take from or give supplies to another country's table. Each country should use all the supplies that country is given.

Pass out the supplies to each table. Each country will receive different supplies based on the wealth and level of development of the country. For example, give "Country A" a nice, large sheet of white butcher or art paper, glue, glitter, markers, ribbons, magazines to cut out pictures, scissors, and colored paper. Give this table some candy or a treat to snack on as well. To "Country F" hand out only a small piece of paper and some crayons or colored pencils. The poor countries should have just bare necessities and the rich countries should receive elaborate supplies.

Students will immediately begin to notice the disparity in the kinds and amounts of supplies the different countries are receiving. Simply restate the rules of the activity and encourage each table to make a banner with the resources they are given.

Allow the children about ten minutes to create their banners. Then hang all the banners on the wall. Ask the children to get into their original small groups at this time.

SHARING TIME

Materials

- treats
- Bibles
- large writing pad
- marker
- *Mrs. Rose's Garden* by Elaine Greenstein

A. DISCOVERING CONTEMPORARY IDEAS ABOUT SHARING THE EARTH'S RESOURCES

Sharing My Life (5–10 minutes)

Purpose

To give children the opportunity to discuss their experiences of the inequity of distribution of resources

Opening Small Group Questions

Debrief the exercise as a small group, discussing the following questions (go ahead and hand out candy or the rich country treats to everyone):

1. What was that activity like? What were you asked to do? What were the rules?

2. How did this exercise make you feel?

3. Did you think it was fair how the different "countries" had very different materials?

4. For those who were part of a rich country, how did it feel to have so many nice materials? Did you enjoy making your banner? How did you feel when you saw the materials the poor countries had?

5. For those that were part of a poor country, how did it feel to have just a few materials? How did you feel when you saw the rich countries eating a treat?

6. How is this exercise like real life in the world in how many resources different countries have (food, energy, material possessions such as clothing, houses, cars, toys, books, and so on)?

7. Does how much we use affect how much the rest of the world has? If so, how?

Wrap up by saying that today we are going to be learning about different ways we can live more simply and reduce how many resources we use so there will be more resources for others.

B. Sharing Others' Experiences of Sharing the Earth's Resources (15–30 minutes)

Purpose

Sharing what we have with others can give a greater sense of satisfaction than keeping everything for ourselves.

Procedure

Say to the children, "When someone comes to stay at your house (perhaps your cousin or grandmother), what kinds of things do you share with them?" (Possible answers include toys, bed, food.) "How does it make you feel to share your toys, food, and other things? Is it easy to give up your things and share them? Have you ever been to a friend's house, and your friend did not want to share their toys with you? If so, how did that make you feel?"

After giving the children time to reply, read the book *Mrs. Rose's Garden* by Elaine Greenstein.

Questions for Discussion

1. At the beginning of this story, what did Mrs. Rose want more than anything else in the world? (To win a blue ribbon)

2. When she knew she would win all the blue ribbons, was she as happy as she thought she would be?

3. What did Mrs. Rose decide to do?

4. Why do you think she decided to do this?

5. What happened because she did this?

6. What do you think about what she did?

B. DISCOVERING A BIBLICAL VIEW ABOUT SHARING THE EARTH'S RESOURCES

Say to the children, "Sometimes it can be hard to share because we are afraid that there may not be enough for us. Let's see what the writer of Matthew says about that."
Read Matthew 6:25–34 as a group.

Questions for Discussion

1. What can we learn from these verses?

2. According to these verses, what would God want us to do?

3. Why do you think God does not want us to worry about having enough food, clothing, and stuff? (See especially verse 33.)

4. Do you think that you have enough food, clothing, and things? Do you have just the right amount, too little, or more than you need?

5. Do you think it is okay to have more than enough food, clothing, and things while someone else does not have enough? Why or why not?

6. Do you think that God wants some people to have a lot while other people do not have enough to survive?

7. Do you think if you were to share some of what you have with someone else that you would still have as much as you need? Why or why not?

Say to the group, "It is hard to focus on living for God and caring about others when we are focusing on having more things for ourselves. Living more simply allows us to focus more on God and helping others. Can you think of some ways that you can live more simply with less stuff?"
Ask the children to list some things that they have too much of that they could give away to someone who needs it more.

C. ENCOURAGING CHILDREN'S CREATIVITY (15–30 minutes)

Purpose

To begin thinking about ways to reduce water consumption

Materials

- poster board
- magazines
- glue
- scissors
- markers

Procedure

Give a piece of poster board, a marker, and scissors to each child. Put magazines and glue within easy reach. Say, "One natural resource that everyone needs is water. Learning to use water carefully is a good way to begin to live a simpler life. This activity will help us start thinking about how we use water and how we can save water."

Instruct the children to draw a line down the middle of their poster board and to label the left side "How I Use Water" and the right side "How I Can Save Water." Ask the children to think about how they use water. Instruct them to cut out pictures from the magazines that show ways water is used. They should glue these pictures on the left side of the board. Then ask them to think about how they can save water. Ask them to glue or draw pictures on the right side to show ways to conserve water. Give the children an opportunity to share what they have created with the group.

Point out that an important way to save water is to buy fewer things. Everything that is manufactured takes lots of water to make.

ACTIVITY TIME

A. HOW PEOPLE IN OTHER COUNTRIES GET AND USE WATER (10–15 minutes)

Purpose

Water is a natural resource that is becoming increasingly scarce. Although in the United States we rarely have to think much about where our water comes from or how clean it is, children in other parts of the world live with a much different situation. The following activities will introduce children to how a child gets water in another country and will give them experiences in conserving water.

Materials

- *Our World of Water* by Beatrice Hollyer
- world map or globe

Advanced Preparation

Copy the following questions on a notecard to guide your discussion:

1. What is the name of the child in our story?
2. Where does this child live?
3. What is the weather like there?
4. How does this child and his family use water?
5. Where does their water come from?
6. Does the child or other family member have to carry water for the family to use?
7. How long does it take?
8. Is the water clean?
9. Do they ever have trouble getting water?

Procedure

Show the map or globe to the children and say, "We are going to read about a child who lives in Ethiopia. Let's find that on the map/globe." Guide children to first find the United States in the continent of North America. Then ask if anyone knows where the continent of Africa is. From there, together you can search for Ethiopia.

As you read *Our World of Water* by Beatrice Hollyer, give the children a chance to look at the photographs. Use the questions you copied earlier to help you discuss the story as you read to the children.

Next, ask the children if anything about this child's life surprised them. Sometimes, children are reluctant to admit that they were surprised, but they may open up if you talk about something that surprised you.

FUN FACT: REPAIRING A FAUCET THAT DRIPS ONE DROP PER SECOND WILL SAVE 2,700 GALLONS EACH YEAR.

Help the children think of ways that the boy from Ethiopia is like them. It may help children develop empathy for others if they see such similarities.

B. WATER WALK (5–10 minutes; longer if done as a relay)

Purpose

While having fun, children also develop a greater appreciation for the difficulty of hauling water.

Note: If you plan to do the car wash (Activity F), save the water you collect from this activity. Otherwise, find a use for the water, such as watering plants.

Materials

- two large containers
- several buckets
- hose
- access to water
- chalk

Advanced Preparation

1. Use the chalk to mark a starting line.

2. Place an empty, large container behind the line.

3. Place another large container at the opposite end of your course. The distance should be far enough that children begin to understand the difficulty of carrying water, but not so far that they don't have fun.

4. Fill the second large container with water.

Procedure

Remind children that, in some places, people don't have water in their homes and have to walk long distances to find water. Often it is the job of the children to carry the water. This activity will give them a chance to see what that might feel like.

Children stand behind the starting line with an empty bucket. They carry the bucket to the opposite end and fill it with water. They then return to the starting line and empty the water into the large container.

Note: You can turn this into a relay by having multiple empty containers at the start line and racing to see which team fills theirs first or fills theirs the most in a given amount of time.

C. HOW TO BRUSH YOUR TEETH (5–10 minutes)

Purpose

To demonstrate how much water is wasted if it runs while you brush your teeth (Kids have probably heard that they should turn the water off while brushing their teeth, but it might be easier for them to remember if they can see why.)

Note: If you plan to do the car wash (Activity F), save the water you collect from this activity. Otherwise, find a use for the water, such as watering plants.

Materials

- five or six empty gallon milk jugs
- timer
- sink
- helper

Procedure

Gather a small group of children around a sink. Tell them, "Today we are talking about ways to save water by not wasting it. Now we are going to look at an activity that people do two or three times a day. Can you guess what it is?"

"Sometimes when people brush their teeth, they forget to turn the water off. That water goes right down the drain."

Show the children a gallon jug. Ask them, "If we let the water run, how many gallons do you think will go down the drain? Okay, let's find out."

Put a jug under the faucet and set the timer for two minutes. Remind children that two minutes is how long they should brush their teeth. Turn the faucet on. Let the children pretend to brush their teeth.

As the jug fills, replace it with the next jug. Continue until the timer goes off. How many gallons did you fill?

Give children a chance to respond to the activity.

D. FOLLOW-UP TO "HOW TO BRUSH YOUR TEETH" (5–10 minutes)

Purpose

To make a reminder to turn off the water while brushing teeth

Materials

- card stock or cereal boxes
- clear contact paper (optional)
- hole punch
- yarn
- markers
- sample messages (following *Procedure*)

Advanced Preparation

Cut the card stock small enough to be hung from a knob in a bathroom.

Write sample messages on a sheet of paper that can be displayed for everyone in the group to see.

Procedure

Distribute cards and markers among the children. Instruct them to copy one of the sample messages about conserving water. They can decorate the card as well.

(Optional) If you have access to a laminating machine, you can laminate the cards, or cover them with clear contact paper.

Punch two holes at the top of the card and string the yarn through so that the card can be hung. Tell the children to hang their signs on a knob in the bathroom as a reminder to save water.

Sample messages:

- Save water: Turn it off while you brush!
- Help the earth: Turn off the water!
- Don't let good water go down the drain: Turn it off!
- Brush your teeth with the water off.

E. MAKE A WATER FILTER (10–15 minutes)

Purpose

To demonstrate that dirty water can be filtered into clean water. CAUTION: This activity will not purify water enough to drink. Please supervise children.

Materials

- empty plastic containers, such as butter tubs, enough for each child and a few extras
- large weave mesh bags, such as onion bags
- rocks
- pebbles
- sand
- cotton balls
- duct tape
- dirt
- empty water bottles or cups, enough for a small group
- bucket
- masking tape or duct tape

Advanced Preparation

1. Prepare a container for each child by cutting a hole in the bottom.
2. Line the container with the mesh and tape it securely.
3. Fill the bucket with water and add dirt.

Procedure

Tell children that not everyone in the world can turn on a faucet and get clean water. Some people only have dirty water to drink, which can make them sick. But if they can filter their water, it will be clean and safe to drink.

Say: "We are going to make our own filters to see how well we can clean dirty water." IMPORTANT: Remind children that their filters will not clean the water enough to drink. They are NOT to drink the water.

Give each child a prepared container. Lay the various filtering materials out where they can reach them. Children should choose the materials they want and layer them in the container in the order they like.

Once filters are prepared, give each child a bottle or cup filled with dirty water. Instruct them to hold their filters over an empty container and pour the water into the filter.

How well did their filters work? Children can compare their results to see which materials and layering worked best. If time permits, allow children to try different combinations.

F. CAR WASH

Purpose

To learn how to conserve water when washing a car

Note 1: Turn this activity into a service project. Children can wash their parents' cars for a fee. The money can be used for a water project, such as buying filters or digging wells.

Note 2: Washing cars in your driveway has two environmental impacts. The first is the use of resources, including water. The second is the contamination of the water supply when polluted water flows into storm drains.

This activity addresses the waste of water. To control contamination, in the future consider a professional car wash or try a waterless car wash product.

Materials

- An environmentally friendly cleaner, such as Biokleen All Purpose Cleaner or Dr. Bonner's Sal Suds.
- hose with an automatic shut-off valve
- sponges or washcloths
- reusable towels

Procedure

Add cleaner to the water saved from Activity B, "Water Walk," or Activity C, "How to Brush Your Teeth." If a car is especially covered with mud, quickly hose it off. Otherwise, just have the children begin to wash, using sponges soaked in the cleaning water.

After the car is sudsed up, quickly hose it off. Have the group towel the car dry.

SUMMARY AND CLOSING (10–15 minutes)

Debriefing in Small Groups

Use the following questions to guide the discussion:

1. What was your favorite activity that you did today?

2. Why did you like this activity so much?

3. What is something that you learned today?

4. In the "Rich Countries, Poor Countries" activity, did anyone want to share their materials with the poor countries?

5. Why do you think it is important to live more simply, using fewer natural resources and products?

6. Do you think you can learn to live a simpler life?

7. What is one way you will live more simply when you go home?

CLOSING PRAYER

Dear God: Even as we give thanks for the good things of the earth that we enjoy, help us to always remember those who have so much less. And when possible, help us to share so that those in other communities and other countries can enjoy more of the earth's good things too. Amen.

Appendix

LETTERS FOR PARENTS

LESSON ONE LETTER TO PARENTS

Dear Parents,

Thank you for sharing your child with us today. This week we will be focusing on our planet and our responsibilities as its citizens. Each day we'll send home a letter to let you know what we've done, so you can continue at home the learning your child has begun.

The title of our lesson today was "Amazement for God's Creation." Our scripture text was Psalm 148:1–12, and our verse of the day was, "God saw everything that he had made, and it was very good" (Genesis 1:31).

During the week, you can continue to help your child develop familiarity with the Bible by looking up the scriptures together. Our goal today was to explore with your child a few of the fascinating animals with whom we share the earth. Our hope is that as children learn more about the earth, they will develop a respect and love for it that will lead to a desire to take care of it.

The animals we learned about today were the blue whale, the polar bear, the hummingbird, the octopus, and the bald eagle. If the opportunity arises, talk with your child about these animals. Here are some questions you might ask:

1. Is the blue whale big? (It's the largest animal ever to live on the earth.)

2. How does the polar bear stand living at the North Pole?

3. Can the hummingbird beat its wings fast? (60 times a second)

4. Does the octopus taste with a tongue? (No, it tastes with the suction cups on its arms.)

5. Could you sit in a bald eagle nest?

Here are some additional questions that you might discuss based on today's Bible studies:

1. What are some things in God's creation that amaze you?

2. What is your favorite thing in God's creation?

3. What is something in nature that makes you think about God?

4. How does seeing the beautiful and amazing things in creation make you feel about God?

Or you could simply let your child share with you what he or she learned.

We would encourage you to continue exploring with your child the wonders of our world. The public library has some good books, both fiction and nonfiction. Visit the zoo. Or simply help your child notice the nature that surrounds them. Put a piece of fruit on the sidewalk and watch the ants that come.

We look forward to seeing you tomorrow!

LESSON TWO LETTER TO PARENTS

Dear Parents,

The title for today's lesson was "Respect for God's Creation." Our scripture texts were Psalm 24:1–2 and Psalm 8, and our verse of the day was, "The earth is the Lord's" (Psalm 24:1).

Our goal was to help children begin to see that everything on the earth is connected, that our actions affect not just ourselves, but other living things as well. It's learning to look at the big picture.

Among our activities, we made alligators and gator holes, experimented with wetlands, and wove a tangled web of connectedness. We shared the books *Who Lives in an Alligator Hole?* by Anne Rockwell and *The Wolves Are Back* by Jean Craighead George. Today, we also had a special treat, a guest speaker from [fill in the blank, depending on who your speaker was].

If the opportunity arises, you might talk with your child about some of these ideas:

1. Why is an alligator important? And who does live in a gator hole?

2. What does a wetland do when it rains? (It soaks up the rain and prevents flooding.)

3. Are animals and plants connected to each other?

Here are some questions you might discuss with your child, based on today's Bible studies:

1. What does the Bible teach us about the earth and everything in it? (To whom does it belong?)

2. How do you think God would like us to treat creation, everything and everyone that lives on the earth?

3. What do you think it means to "respect" creation?

Or you could simply let your child share with you what he or she learned.

Learning to understand the impact of our actions on the environment can be a lifelong project. As you make your own decisions to lighten your impact, share your thinking with your child. No one is a better teacher or model than you.

We look forward to seeing you tomorrow!

LESSON THREE LETTER TO PARENTS

Dear Parents,

The title today was "Keepers of God's Creation." Our scripture text was Genesis 2:8–9 and 15, and our verse of the day was, "God put the man and woman in the garden to keep it." (Genesis. 2:15).

Our goal today was to introduce children to some simple ways that they can help take care of the earth by recycling and reusing its resources and replacing inefficient items. Among our activities, we explored energy consuming and energy efficient items, learned what kinds of things are recyclable, dove into a pile of garbage, made paper pads from used paper, sewed quilt blocks from scraps, made new paper from old, turned old greeting cards into new, and used comics for gift wrap.

The book we shared was *Something from Nothing* by Phoebe Gilman. This is a story about a grandfather who was a master of reusing old, worn clothes to make something new.

If the opportunity arises, you might talk with your child about some of these ideas:

1. What kinds of things can we recycle?

2. Did you make something new from something used? Tell me about it.

3. What are some things we can do to help take care of the earth?

Here are some questions you might discuss with your child, based on today's Bible studies:

1. Who do you think God wants to take care of creation?

2. What do you think it means to take care of creation?

3. What is one of your ideas for how we can cut down on our energy consumption at home?

4. What are two of your ideas for how we can recycle and reuse things more at home?

Or you could simply let your child share with you what he or she learned.

Help your child look at his or her actions and find ways to conserve resources. Learning good habits from the start is much easier than trying to break bad habits later!

We look forward to seeing you tomorrow!

LESSON FOUR LETTER TO PARENTS

Dear Parents,

The lesson title today was "Care and Repair of God's Creation." Our scripture texts were Genesis 1:26–31a and Romans 8:21–22. Our verse of the day was, "Be fruitful and multiply and fill the earth" (Genesis 1:28).

Whereas yesterday we looked at ways to prevent problems through simple steps like recycling, reducing, and replacing, today we looked at how we can begin to replenish and repair some problems that we've created. We approached this positively, with the idea that even one person can make a difference and that, if we work together, we can solve problems.

Our activities included making a giant "Thank You!" for trees, exploring and planting seeds, cleaning up an oil spill (vegetable oil and cocoa!), cleaning (pretend) animals caught in an oil spill, and playing a litter race game. We also made a special trip to a nearby neighbor to plant a tree.

The book we shared was *A River Ran Wild* by Lynn Cherry, a story about how one person's dream of a clean river made a difference.

If the opportunity arises, you might talk with your child about some of these ideas:

1. What does oil do on water? (It floats.) What are some ways of getting the oil out of the water?

2. Tell me about your sock animal. What happened to it?

3. Why should we plant seeds and trees?

Here are some questions you might discuss with your child, based on today's Bible studies:

1. How do you think God feels about creation?

2. What are some things in creation that God gives all people to take care of?

3. In what ways do you think the earth is sick or broken?

4. Can you think of some ways that we can help replenish or repair the earth's resources?

Or you could simply let your child share with you what he/she learned.

Some of the earth's environmental problems are massive. As parents, we have to decide what is appropriate for our kids to know. Look for simple ways to share with your child the idea of responsibility, such as picking up litter. Share news stories and books about people who are making a difference. Plant the seeds of change to grow with your child.

We look forward to seeing you tomorrow!

LESSON FIVE LETTER TO PARENTS

Dear Parents,

The lesson title today was "Consumption of God's Creation." Our scripture text was Exodus 16:4–8, 13–21. Our verse of the day was, "Use only what you need" (based on Exodus 16:16).

Our goal today was to help children begin to develop awareness of what they consume and look for ways to reduce. Our activities included packing a suitcase, making an honest commercial, learning to cut paper without waste, and exploring the heating power of the sun and the insulating power of wool.

We shared the book *One Potato, Two Potato* by Cynthia DeFelice, a story about a couple who used a magic pot to fulfill their needs without greed.

If the opportunity arises, you might talk with your child about some of these ideas:

1. What things did you pack in your suitcase (what is the difference between a necessity and a luxury)?

2. Tell me about your commercial?

3. Did your ice cube melt faster in the sun or the shade?

4. Why should you wear a sweater in the winter?

Here are some questions you might discuss with your child, based on today's Bible studies:

1. What happened in the story about God's people when God gave the people bread from heaven each morning? What happened when they tried to collect too much?

2. Why do you think God wants us to take and use only what we need and not too much?

3. Can you think of something at home that we can try using just as much as we need and not too much?

Or you could simply let your child share with you what he or she learned.

Children can be impulsive buyers and may find it hard to resist the lure of advertisements. It may help them reduce their consumption by having a "cooling off" period before a purchase: let your child think about a purchase for a day or two. Sometimes they'll even forget they wanted it in the first place.

Also, help your child look for ways to reduce at home. Remind him or her to turn off lights and be careful about wasting water.

We look forward to seeing you tomorrow!

Lesson Six Letter to Parents

Dear Parents,

Today was the final day of our camp. We have enjoyed this time of getting to know your child and sharing ideas about taking care of the earth. Thank you for helping your child be a part.

Our lesson title today was "Living in God's Creation." Our scripture text was Matthew 6:25–34 and 7:12. Our verse of the day was, "Do not worry about your life" (Matthew 6:25).

Our goal today built on our lesson about reducing. Today, we looked at how reducing our consumption helps not only the earth, but also other people who have less than we do.

Our activities began with an exercise in which some of us had less than others. We then focused on conserving one very important resource—water. We compared our experience with water to that of a child in Ethiopia, felt the difficulty of hauling water, learned how to brush our teeth without wasting water, and tried our hand at making water filters.

The book we shared was *Mrs. Rose's Garden* by Elaine Greenstein, in which Mrs. Rose learns that sharing what you have can give a greater sense of satisfaction than keeping everything for yourself. We also used the book *Our World of Water* by Beatrice Hollyer.

If the opportunity arises, you might talk with your child about some of these ideas:

1. Does everyone in the world have as much as we do?

2. Can everyone get clean water out of a faucet?

3. What are some ways we can save water?

4. Was it easy to carry a bucket of water?

Here are some questions you might discuss with your child, based on today's Bible studies:

1. Why do you think God does not want us to worry about having enough food, clothing, or stuff?

2. How do you think God feels when some people have too much and others do not have enough?

3. Do you think we have enough food, clothing, and things?

4. If we were to share some things with other people who do not have enough, do you think that we would still have enough?

5. Can you think of something that we have too much of that we could share with someone else?

Or you could simply let your child share with you what he/she learned.

If you are old enough, you may remember your parents telling you to eat all your food because children were starving in China. And as a child, you may have been completely perplexed by how eating your peas would help a starving child on the other side of the world. Similarly, it is difficult to see how our conserving water and reducing consumption will help a child in Africa. Indeed, the line is not a straight one and there are political, economical, and geographical complications, even to the point that it's hard to know the right thing to do.

Just as with environmental problems, parents need to decide what is appropriate for their children to know about other cultures. In the meantime, look for opportunities to share other cultures with your child. The library should have some great books about children in other countries. Also, you may find local opportunities for your child to help others, such as giving to a Christmas toy drive. And share your actions with your child. If you give to charities that help the environment or people less fortunate, let you child know you do this and why you think it is important.

Together, we have planted seeds of change. Let's continue to nurture them and watch them grow!

Resource List

CHAPTER ONE

Adams, Ansel. *The Portfolios of Ansel Adams*. Boston: New York Graphic Society, 1981.
_____. *Yosemite*. Boston: Little, Brown, 1995.
_____. *Yosemite and the High Sierra*. Boston: Little, Brown, 1994.
_____. *Yosemite and the Range of Light*. Boston: Little, Brown, 1992.
Ernst, Lisa Campbell. *Round Like a Ball*. Maplewood: Blue Apple Books, 2008.
McGinty, Alice B. *Thank You, World*. Illustrated by Wendy Anderson Halperin. New York: Dial, 2007.
New Century Hymnal. Cleveland: Pilgrim Press, 1995.
Nichols, Judith, compiler. *The Sun in Me: Poems about the Planet*. Illustrated by Beth Krommes. Cambridge: Barefoot Books, 2003.
Thomson, Richard. *Vincent van Gogh: The Starry Night*. New York: Museum of Modern Art, 2008.
Walther, Ingo F., and Rainer Metzger. *Vincent van Gogh: The Complete Paintings*. Köln: Benedikt Taschen, 1990.

CHAPTER TWO

America's National Parks. New York: Crescent Books, 1993.
George, Jean Craighead. *The Wolves Are Back*. Paintings by Wendell Minor. New York: Dutton's Children's Books, 2008.
Locker, Thomas. *John Muir: America's Naturalist*. Golden: Fulcrum Publishing, 2003.
Marshall, Janet. *Banana Moon*. New York: Greenwillow Books, 1998.
New Century Hymnal. Cleveland: Pilgrim Press, 1995.
Rockwell, Anne. *Who Lives in an Alligator Hole?* Illustrated by Lizzy Rockwell. New York: Collins, 2006.
Sharratt, Nick. *Shark in the Park*. New York: D. Fickling Books, 2003.

CHAPTER THREE

Gilman, Phoebe. *Something from Nothing.* New York: Scholastic, 1992.

New Century Hymnal. Cleveland: Pilgrim Press, 1995.

Taback, Simms. *Joseph Had a Little Overcoat.* New York: Penguin Putnam Books for Young Readers, 1999.

CHAPTER FOUR

Cherry, Lynne. *A River Ran Wild: An Environmental History.* San Diego: Harcourt Brace Jovanovich, 1992.

DePalma, Mary Newell. *A Grand Old Tree.* New York: Arthur A. Levine Books, 2005.

New Century Hymnal. Cleveland: Pilgrim Press, 1995.

Tresselt, Alvin. *The Gift of the Tree.* Illustrated by Henri Sorensen. New York: Lothrop, Lee and Shepard, 1992.

CHAPTER FIVE

DeFelice, Cynthia. *One Potato, Two Potato.* Illustrated by Andrea U'Ren. New York: Farrar, Straus and Giroux, 2006.

New Century Hymnal. Cleveland: Pilgrim Press, 1995.

CHAPTER SIX

Greenstein, Elaine. *Mrs. Rose's Garden.* New York: Simon & Schuster Books for Young Readers, 1996.

Hollyer, Beatrice. *Our World of Water.* New York: Henry Holt, 2009.

New Century Hymnal. Cleveland: Pilgrim Press, 1995.

OTHER BOOKS FROM RANDY HAMMER

THE TALKING STICK
Forty Children's Sermons with Activities

RANDY HAMMER

ISBN 978-0-8298-1761-4 / $15

The Talking Stick is a collection of children's stories or lessons whose topics generally follow the church year beginning in September and ending with Pentecost. An overall aim throughout the stories is to lift up the Divine Image that is planted within each child in order to promote equality, justice, and the inherent worth and dignity of all children. Additionally, it encourages each child to be the best he or she was created to be.

To order these or any other books from The Pilgrim Press call or write to:

THE PILGRIM PRESS
700 PROSPECT AVENUE EAST
CLEVELAND, OHIO 44115-1100

PHONE ORDERS: 1-800-537-3394 ■ FAX ORDERS: 216-736-2206

Please include shipping charges of $6.00 for the first book and $1.00 for each additional book. Or order from our web sites at www.pilgrimpress.com and www.ucpress.com.

Prices subject to change without notice.